Frank Lloyd Wright

Titles in the series Critical Lives present the work of leading cultural figures of the modern period. Each book explores the life of the artist, writer, philosopher or architect in question and relates it to their major works.

In the same series

Michel Foucault
David Macey

Jean Genet
Stephen Barber

Pablo Picasso
Mary Ann Caws

Franz Kafka
Sander L. Gilman

Guy Debord
Andy Merrifield

Marcel Duchamp
Caroline Cros

James Joyce
Andrew Gibson

Jean-Paul Sartre
Andrew Leak

Frank Lloyd Wright

Robert McCarter

REAKTION BOOKS

To Bruce Brooks Pfeiffer

Published by Reaktion Books Ltd
33 Great Sutton Street
London EC1V ODX, UK

www.reaktionbooks.co.uk

First published 2006

Printed and bound in The Netherlands
by Krips B. V.

British Library Cataloguing in Publication Data
McCarter, Robert
 Frank Lloyd Wright. – (Critical lives)
 1. Wright, Frank Lloyd, 1867–1959 2. Wright, Frank Lloyd, 1867–1959 –
 Criticism and interpretation 3. Architects, United States – 20th century
 – Biography 4. Architecture, Modern – 20th century 5. Architecture –
 United States – 20th century
 I. Title
 720.9'2

ISBN 1 86189 268 3

Contents

Frank Lloyd Wright in 1926.

Introduction:
Wright at the Defining Moment

This book examines both the critical events and the defining works
of architecture – and the places, occasions, relationships and ideas
that shaped them – in the life of American architect Frank Lloyd
Wright (1867–1959). Wright's life and architecture have been the
subject of a seemingly endless number of books and writings,
beginning in 1900, when Wright was aged 33, and continuing
unabated to this day, at the beginning of a new century. Yet within
this outpouring the reader will discern a consistent division
between those books that document and analyse his architectural
works, largely excluding any discussion of his daily life, and those
books that tell the often sensational tale of his life, with barely
a passing reference to either the buildings themselves or the
countless hours he spent working on his designs. Also too often
overlooked in existing studies are the ideas and beliefs that shaped
Wright's work, the larger intellectual context in which he worked,
and the manner in which these affected, and are reflected in, his
architecture. The result is that, despite the large number of books
on Wright, the most essential part of his life – his life as an
architect, working, as he said, 'in the cause of architecture' –
remains virtually unexplored. This book, which endeavours to
give an account of Wright's life as an architect, may thus be defined
as *an architectural biography*.

During a life and career that spanned the greater part of the
United States's second century, Wright actively engaged and
endeavoured to shape American democracy's emergence and

evolution in the modern world. Joining ancient place-making geometries to contemporary ideals of Transcendental philosophy, Wright sought to develop an appropriate architecture for both the young American nation and the new world of the twentieth century. Wright believed it was his task to house the experiences of daily life in a new architecture that was formed by integrated conceptions of both collective monumentality and individual dwelling. Wright's work thus redefined our understanding of the city, the ideal of the community, and the nature of the single family house. In this way, Wright's architecture crystallized key conceptions of both private dwelling and public citizenship for the young American society, as well as serving as the primary inspiration for the emergence of Modern architecture around the world.

Today, almost 50 years after his death, Wright remains by far the most widely recognized Modern architect in the world. Though he came to maturity in the nineteenth-century American culture of immigration and Emerson, and was already middle-aged at the turn of the twentieth century, Wright's buildings, and the ideas that underlie them, nevertheless continue to inspire new architecture in the twenty-first century. Wright's architecture is timeless and affects us in a manner that is as aggravating to historians, intent upon chronological, comparative and conceptual categorizations, as it is endearing to the general public, who recognize in Wright's architecture both its appeal to fundamental, unchanging human qualities and its spirited engagement of contemporary life. Wright himself felt that, despite their unparalleled formal, material and spatial variety, all his architectural works originated from the same ordering principles, consistently applied throughout his 72-year career. Frank Lloyd Wright's built works fully embody his ethical ideals for architecture, his conception of democracy founded on both individual and collective integrity, and his vision of modern life in harmony with nature – all of which continue to be as valid today as when he first conceived these exceptional places.

1

Unity and Nature's Geometry
1867–87

Frank Lincoln Wright, so named by his parents William Carey
Wright and Anna Lloyd Jones Wright, was born on 8 June 1867
in Richland Center, Wisconsin. Wright would maintain throughout his life that his date of birth was two years later, and much
has been made of this in biographies of Wright. This includes
the assertion that Wright's life 'starts with a lie',[1] and the equally
questionable claim that this change of birth date was the beginning of Wright's 'lifelong habit of turning fact into fiction'.[2]
In this case, it is perhaps more appropriate to note this as a
very effective example of Wright's turning fiction into fact, for
Wright's revised birth date of 1869 is today, almost 140 years
afterwards, still to be found in many highly respected and
widely employed reference books.

Wright always maintained that he believed his birth date
of 1869 as given by his mother, yet Anna Lloyd Jones had also
changed her own date of birth by four years, from 1838 to 1842.[3]
In her case the motive is fairly clear, for it allowed her to maintain that she was 24 years old at the time of her marriage in 1866,
rather than her true age of 28 – late to be getting married in that
period and place. Wright likely knew from a fairly early age that
his mother had changed the date of his birth, yet he chose to
maintain his public belief in his mother's modified version until
the end of his life, when, just two months shy of his 92nd birthday, he passed away in Phoenix, Arizona. At the time of his death,

preparations were under way for what virtually everyone involved thought would be Wright's 90th birthday party in June.

Even without the two years of added youth, Wright was as precocious an architect as the world had ever known. In no small part this must be credited to the remarkable family, time and place into which he was born. The first significant influence on Wright's early development was his mother's extraordinary family, the Lloyd Joneses, a Celtic clan of religious revolutionaries who had broken away from the established Protestant church during the Methodist revival, and played a part in the founding of the Unitarian sect in Wales in 1726.[4] Considering themselves Nonconformists and Dissenters in their religious practices, the Lloyd Joneses were among the numerous freedom-seeking refugees and rebels from Europe arriving in the New World at this time. From 1840 to 1890 some 15 million immigrants came to America, accounting for one-third of the nation's population increase during that period.

For European immigrants, America offered the possibility of a new beginning, and this appealed particularly to the radical ministers and educators in the Lloyd Jones family, who brought with them a tradition of holding to their own thoughts and beliefs in the face of all opposition. Wright's grandparents, Richard and Mallie Lloyd Jones, emigrated to America in 1844 from Llandysul, Wales, bringing their seven children, Thomas, John, Margaret, Mary, Anna, Nanny and Jenkin. Nanny died during their subsequent travels in search of a homestead, and four more children, James, Enos, Nell and Jane (called Jennie), were born in America. In 1852 the close-knit family began purchasing what would eventually total 1,800 acres of land outside Spring Green, near Madison, along the Wisconsin River. In 1864, as the end of the Civil War approached, the Lloyd Joneses settled in what came to be known as 'The Valley of the God-Almighty Joneses',[5] adopting as their family motto the phrase 'Truth against the world'.

Large family portrait of the Lloyd Jones family, *c.* 1883, in Madison, Wisconsin. The future architect sits to the right of the empty chair.

Traditional Celtic society was structured around close family relations, and a child was considered to belong to his mother's side of the family, rather than to his father's.[6] Without question, Wright's mother's family was of the utmost importance in the shaping of his world-view, as is indicated by his decision at the age of eighteen to change his name from Frank Lincoln Wright to Frank Lloyd Wright, thus becoming a full-fledged member of the clan.

Wright's original middle name of Lincoln likely came from his father, and it was a popular name for children at the time. In April 1865 in Lone Rock, Wisconsin, William Wright had given a highly praised eulogy for Abraham Lincoln following the Civil War president's assassination, and the Lloyd Jones family was deeply committed to the anti-slavery, abolitionist cause. Lincoln would haunt the young American nation for years to come, and Frank Lincoln Wright grew up in a tradition of Unitarian religious practice standing in opposition to slavery that linked his family with that of such New England contemporaries as Henry and William James, novelist and philosopher-psychologist, respectively, and Oliver Wendell Holmes, Supreme Court Justice, as well as the father-figure and founder of American Transcendental philosophy, Ralph Waldo Emerson.

While building their farm houses in the Valley near Spring Green, the Lloyd Jones family lived in Bear Creek, near Lone Rock, and Anna Lloyd Jones worked in the school district of which William Wright was the superintendent. A family story holds that Anna lodged in the Wright household prior to the death of William's first wife, Permelia, in 1863. After their mother's death, William's three young children, Charles, George and Elizabeth, went to live with their maternal grandmother until Anna and William were married in August 1866.

William Wright was of noble English lineage, his family claiming to be descendants of William the Conqueror,[7] and his father was a Baptist minister. William had studied medicine and passed the bar exam to practice law, later establishing himself as an organist, musician and teacher of the keyboard, as well as an educator and public speaker. William had come to Lone Rock in 1859 as a lawyer, and later was elected school superintendent. When he met Anna, William was studying for the ministry, which he subsequently took up as yet another occupation. At the time of their marriage, Anna was 28 and William 42, and they would have three children together, making six altogether with his three children from his first marriage.

In May 1867 Anna and William moved to Richland Center, about 30 kilometres from Spring Green, where William, newly ordained as a minister, was to oversee construction of the Central Baptist Society's new building. One month later their son Frank was born, followed in the next years by his sisters Jane and Maginel. William Wright was by all accounts quite popular, involved in both the political and moral life of the communities where he served as minister. He was an accomplished musician, giving highly praised recitals, and a public speaker able to lecture on a wide variety of subjects. In fact, it is clear that William was skilled at almost anything he put his mind to do, with the glaring exceptions of continuous employment and making a living.

Wright's family moved five times over the next ten years, when he was two, four, six, seven, and ten years of age: to MacGregor, Iowa (on the Mississippi River); Pawtucket, Rhode Island; Essex, Connecticut; Weymouth, Massachusetts; and finally to Madison, Wisconsin. Each time they arrived in a new town William made a good first impression and often a successful start, but thereafter proved incapable of securing adequate financial support for his family, forcing them to move again soon in search of better opportunity. Each move meant the pain of parting, and yet also a new place, new friends and new opportunities. Wright learned to make new friends and to engage new places; while these relationships were denied the luxury of longevity, they possessed an unusual intensity of feeling.

The situation of the Wright family was hardly unique, however, for in the 1870s the nation was in the midst of a severe economic depression that coincided with the fire in Chicago of 1871 and that city's subsequent rebuilding, and small towns often could not provide sufficient funding for their church and its pastor, despite the best of intentions. Wright's memories of what was without question an impoverished childhood included living in various small crowded houses, strenuously pumping the bellows until the tears flowed while his father played the church organ, as well as the all too common 'donation parties', where everything from second-hand clothing to pies were given to the Wrights by the congregation in a doomed effort to keep them in town.

Despite these hardships, during the eighteen years he lived with his father Wright developed a deep and abiding love of music, a marked talent for playing the piano, an understanding of musical composition as a creative act (watching his father go back and forth from piano to writing table, his pen held in his teeth while he played), the memorization of much of Bach and Beethoven by listening to his father playing the piano late into the night, and his own daily practice of Schubert, Mendelssohn and Czerny's

Exercises, among others. While the family remained poverty-stricken throughout Wright's youth, there was always a piano (if not much else) in his home, and later in life he would return to playing the piano as both a way to establish his presence in a strange place – even in the Arizona desert at a makeshift camp – and as rejuvenation from arduous labour during the long nights of working at the drawing board. As Wright said of his father, 'He had his music still, which always consoled him, and music was his friend to the last when all else had failed.'[8]

Wright inherited from his father a natural skill at a wide variety of tasks, a stubborn self-assurance and a seemingly unfailing self-confidence in public presentations. Combined with the skills at making friends and adapting rapidly to new situations forced upon him by his family's constant moves from state to state, these traits can be counted among the reasons Wright would later be recognized as the only modern architect with a commanding and captivating public presence equal to famous contemporary cultural and political figures. On the other hand, Wright also inherited his father's inability to manage the family finances, his habit of spending money on luxuries rather than necessities, his tendency to make exaggerated claims and occasional distortions of the truth, and his penchant for avoiding rather than confronting difficult situations.

From both his father and mother Wright inherited an all-consuming love of reading (books were the family's most prized possessions) and he recalls reading the works of Emerson, William Channing, Theodore Parker, Henry David Thoreau, John Ruskin, Johann Wolfgang von Goethe, Henry Wadsworth Longfellow, Percy Bysshe Shelley, Edgar Allen Poe, Thomas Carlyle, Edward Gibbon, Plutarch, Jules Verne, Victor Hugo, James Russell Lowell, William Blake, Eugene-Emmanuel Viollet-le-Duc, as well as *The Arabian Nights* (Wright's nickname for himself at this time was 'Aladdin') and dozens of 'Nickel Library' mysteries, ghost stories and thrillers.

This was complemented by Wright's early interest in printing and typography (he set up a printing press 'business' with his closest friend in Madison, Robie Lamp, a cripple without the use of his legs), in making all manner of inventions and in drawing. From his earliest memories Wright describes himself as perpetually making drawings: drawings for inventions, drawings of nature, drawings as a way to exercise the imagination – he was always drawing, especially in the evenings by lamplight.

Most histories have made little of his father's influence, instead emphasizing his mother's claim to have predetermined her only son to be an architect – including hanging etchings of English Gothic cathedrals above his crib before he was born. It may well have been the high esteem in which her oldest brother Thomas, a self-made carpenter and builder, was held by the Lloyd Joneses of the Valley, that made architecture seem a suitably noble profession towards which to direct her eldest child and only son. Anna's intense desire for Frank to be a success resulted in her placing wildly excessive expectations and demands on him, as well as in her obsessive dedication to him from his infancy until her own death. Yet Wright would in the end emerge as a complex blend of both his father and mother, in all their best and worst traits.

Eventually the pattern of nomadic family life and ever-insufficient means led to the slow deterioration of Anna and William's marriage. After their move back to Madison in 1877, probably supported by the Lloyd Jones family, comfortably settled in the Valley, William again pursued a series of apparently unprofitable jobs, including establishing a conservatory of music. While the Wright family lived in Madison for eight years, far longer than they had stayed in any other place, the marriage nevertheless began to fail soon after their arrival, with her demanding more financial support than he was able to provide and then denying him conjugal relations, starting in 1883. Years before, Anna had begun to favour her own children, denying attention and affection to William's children from his former marriage.

As a result of all the escalating tensions and conflicts between them, William began to withdraw more and more from the family, and Frank assumed that his parents' frequent heated differences were over him, that perhaps he was the cause, as is typical in such situations.

When his parents' split finally came, in 1885, Wright would accept his mother's story, claiming that his father abandoned the family; in fact it was his father who instigated the divorce proceedings, charging spousal abuse and abandonment. In the divorce proceedings William stated that Anna said she hated the very ground he walked on,[9] and it was Anna's bitterness that finally drove him away. Wright never saw his father again, nor did he attend William's funeral in Lone Rock in 1904, although in later years he did make solitary visits to the grave. Anna and her three children remained in the house in Madison, on Lake Mendota, 60 kilometres from the Valley of the Lloyd Joneses, and it was around this time that the eighteen-year-old changed his name to Frank Lloyd Wright.

Wherever his family happened to be living at the time, each summer during his childhood Wright returned to visit his Lloyd Jones relatives in the Valley, along the Wisconsin River. Thus the area was already quite familiar to Wright at the age of ten when his family moved back to Madison, after which he spent every summer working on the farm of his uncle, James Lloyd Jones. Wright recalled the exhausting labour of farm life, getting up early and working hard all day long, which he described as 'adding tired to tired'.[10] The experience of eight summers spent on his uncle's farm, the discipline for hard work it instilled in him, and the opportunity it provided him to spend long hours in nature, were to have a profound and lasting effect on Wright, resulting in his great love of and respect for the formative powers of nature.

Nature – capitalized to signify that it was Wright's church, the place where he worshipped God in His works – would become for Wright both the inspiration and the measure of all his own works.

This was reinforced from an early age by Anna's favourite quotation from Shakespeare, from *As You Like It*: 'And this our life, exempt from public haunt, finds tongues in trees, books in the running brooks, sermons in stones, and good in everything.'[11] As an additional prompting of Anna's decision to will Frank to become an architect, we should note that this quotation combines the idea of nature as the source of all that is good, and the definition of architecture as 'sermons in stones' – a phrase surely freighted with meaning for a family of preachers such as the Lloyd Joneses.

For Wright, Sundays in the Valley were his salvation from 'adding tired to tired', when it was his responsibility to rise early and decorate the pulpit of the family chapel with blooms and branches he collected from the hillsides. His uncle, Jenkin Lloyd Jones, who at this time was emerging as the most famous Unitarian minister in the world, would preach a sermon and read from the Transcendental classics of Emerson and Thoreau, as well as from the poetry of Longfellow and Lowell, and at the end the children would sing. Uncle Thomas would then take them on a picnic in the woods and fields that opened in every direction.

Every summer Jenkin Lloyd Jones would raise a tent in the Valley and host a Unitarian Chautauqua, educational gatherings at which the speakers eventually included progressive politicians such as Robert La Follette, settlement house founder Jane Addams, women's suffrage leader Susan B. Anthony, as well as other religious leaders, such as William C. Gannett, a leading Unitarian from Chicago. Years later Wright would collaborate with Gannett on the design and printing of *The House Beautiful*, the text of which is a sermon on that subject by Jenkin Lloyd Jones. The Unitarianism of the Lloyd Joneses, as the young Wright understood it, was an attempt to emphasize, amidst the competing creeds of the day, 'the idea of life as a gift from a divine source', with nature exemplifying the perfect works of God. Wright was raised in the Welsh branch of the Unitarian faith, with the ideal of *unity*, 'the UNITY of all things!'[12] understood to be the beginning and the end of all humankind's efforts to achieve truth – and beauty, Wright would later say.

In *An Autobiography* Wright recalls how his reverence for nature and the ideal of unity were reinforced and transformed into constructive method through the Froebel kindergarten training introduced to him by his mother. In 1876, while the Wright family was living in Weymouth, Massachusetts, Anna and her teacher sisters, Jane and Nell, visited the Centennial Exposition held in Philadelphia, celebrating the first 100 years of the American nation. There the three sisters were able to examine a display of the kindergarten 'gifts' and instructions for teachers developed by Friedrich Froebel. Soon after returning from Philadelphia Anna made a trip to Boston, to the Milton Bradley store, to purchase a set of Froebel 'gifts' for use in educating the three Wright children, including the first English translation of the all-important teaching manuals, which had been published in 1874, only two years earlier.

Froebel had begun his own education studying science in the field of crystallography, the study of the geometry of rock crystal formations. He later studied architecture for two years and finally became a teacher. From 1807 to 1809 he worked with Johann Pestalozzi, whose experimental school emphasized the principle of teaching and learning through the child's voluntary activities. Froebel's own methods, described in the instructional manuals that accompanied his training 'gifts', consisted of both philosophical and formal ordering principles imparted to the child through a series of twenty 'gifts', spatial and tactile (rather than written) instruments of learning, a number of which were developed from crystallography. These 'gifts' were to be given to the child in a predetermined sequence, ideally starting at infancy and finishing at age five, although the pace at which the child moved through the 'gifts' was largely self-determined.

Wright was first given the Froebel 'gifts' and their accompanying orchestrated training by his mother at the advanced age of nine. While this fact has often been used to cast doubt on the impact of the Froebel training on Wright's architectural capacities, if we examine the twenty 'gifts' and their matching instruction manuals, with their rhetoric of unity in all things and learning from natural forms, one might well conclude that the impact on Wright at age nine was far greater than it would have been had they been introduced to him in infancy. Given his love of nature, his being raised under the influence of both Unitarianism and Transcendentalism, and his desire to learn by doing, the nine-year-old Wright was in fact an ideal subject for Froebel training. Unlike those introduced to it in infancy, Wright was old enough to comprehend fully both the diagrams and the words in the teacher's guides, which every afternoon his mother lay open before her as they worked with the 'gifts' on the low table.

First and foremost, Froebel training emphasized learning from nature, which reinforced and gave order to Wright's early experiences on his uncle's farm. Equally important, it taught him *how to see*, how to discern the geometric shapes that lay hidden beneath external appearances, structuring every natural and manmade thing – to see each thing 'in its organic unity', as Froebel himself explained in the teaching manual.[13] The training was intended to lead each child, through their own play with the 'gifts', to the understanding that there was an inner coherence in all things, and that the physical and spiritual worlds were one and the same. A non-verbal, non-representational educational system relying on the child's own discoveries through making, the Froebel training began 'by establishing spatial relationships', as Froebel wrote, and was directed primarily towards the development of analytical thinking.

'The smooth shapely maple blocks with which to build, the sense of which never afterwards leaves the fingers: so *form* became *feeling*', as Wright recalled.[14] As this and other of Wright's memories indicate, the Froebel training was predominantly tactile, with the visual aspects of colour and shape being far less emphasized than in traditional educational methods. While the wooden blocks are likely all that the modern world knows of the Froebel training, they in fact made up only four of the twenty 'gifts', with largest number, nine, being weaving exercises, including interlaced slats and rings, woven paper strips and sewing. The balance was made up of fundamental forms for infancy, drawing, pin-pricking, parquetry, peas as joints for framing, and the last, modelling clay, with which one could make any form imaginable. Each of the exercises was provided with sample solutions in the teacher's guide, and each used a square-gridded paper or mat as a base for the exercise, as well as square-gridded paper on which the child was to draw and document their constructions.

In having this experience in his childhood, Wright was hardly alone. Froebel training was widely adopted in Europe from 1860 to 1920, affecting early childhood education systems in nearly every country. Recent research has indicated the strong possibility that a significant number of early Modern artists and architects may have benefited from Froebel training, either as a student or teacher, including Georges Braque, Piet Mondrian, Johannes Itten, Josef Albers, Wassily Kandinsky, Paul Klee, Walter Gropius and Le Corbusier, among others.[15] Yet the case of Froebel training's existence and influence is only fully documented with Wright, who in his autobiography describes this experience of his youth and its importance to his development as an architect.

At the very least, Wright's relationship with this early Froebel training must be understood as the fortuitous meeting of an unusually comprehensive and effective method and an astonishing, and perhaps unparalleled, natural talent. As a result of the Froebel training Wright was far more interested in *designing* the world than in *representing* it – designing here understood as discerning the underlying structure of nature and working with it. Despite occasional scholarly doubt, the Froebel training he received from his mother must in the end be given a prominent place in the early development of Wright's system of design.

This experience found its perfect complement in the profound influence exercised on Wright by Transcendentalism. In considering Wright and his architecture, it is important to remember that, while he would live until 1959, Wright was essentially a nineteenth-century man, already 32 years of age at the turn of the twentieth century, his fundamental principles and beliefs formed by the comprehensive philosophy for living proposed by the Transcendental thinkers – the only truly indigenous culture to appear since the founding of the American nation only 91 years before Wright's birth. Wright's work, therefore, should be seen not as a product of the often doubt-filled and ideal-less twentieth century, but of the energetic and optimistic American transcendental culture of the previous century.

Transcendentalism was an idealistic school of thought prominent in New England from 1830 to 1880, and best represented in the writings of Emerson, who in 1836 had established the Transcendentalist Club. The core group of Transcendentalists included Emerson, Thoreau, Parker, Margaret Fuller (grandmother of Buckminster Fuller) and Bronson Alcott, but their thinking also influenced, and was influenced by, Herman Melville, Walt Whitman and Horatio Greenough. This diverse group of thinkers was united by their origins in the liberal religious tradition of Unitarianism; by their engagement of contemporary European idealistic philosophy and the works of William Wordsworth and Coleridge; by their exploration of non-western philosophies, such as the varied traditions of Oriental spirituality; and by their criticism of contemporary society through beliefs and judgments founded upon each individual's ethical intuition.

Emerson's 1836 essay 'Nature' was the first definitive statement of Transcendental principles, and in all his enormously influential essays Emerson held that because human beings were a product of nature, they were eminently suited to intuit the principles of nature: '. . . the truth was in us before it was reflected back to us from natural objects.'[16] In a manner sympathetic to Froebel training, Emerson emphasized searching for the underlying geometries of nature, 'reasoning from the seen to the unseen'. As a result of both influences, Wright would later analyse nature and its underlying geometric structures, using their purity of form, clarity of purpose and perfect adaptation to place to critique his own architecture.

The Transcendentalists held that each physical thing was the consequence of, and had consequences for, spiritual thought, and that the forms we made were a direct effect of our characters. Wright would later state this more pointedly, saying that '. . . the sins of architects are permanent sins'.[17] For the Transcendentalists, all form had moral meaning, and nature was the model; Emerson held that we should '. . . esteem nature a perpetual counselor, and her perfections the exact measure of our deviations.' Thus for Wright, the philosophical ideals of unity, integrity and natural order were never mere means of designing – they were part of a vision of the world as it should be.

This evolving American culture had a strongly critical aspect, opposed to the attitude of dominating nature that characterized the industrial age, and instead sought to achieve a harmony with nature. Wright displayed the boundless confidence typical of Transcendentalist thinkers that democracy in America could achieve the liberation of the individual, the creation of an indigenous culture, and the dynamic integration of the evolutionary forces, all to be played out across the enormous expanses of the continent. As Charles Olson wrote in his study of Melville's *Moby-Dick*:

> I take SPACE to be the central fact to man born in America, from Folsom cave to now. I spell it large because it comes large

here. Large and without mercy. It is geography at bottom, a hell of a wide land from the beginning. The fulcrum of America is the Plains, half sea half land, a high sun as metal and obdurate as the iron horizon, and a man's job is to square the circle.[18]

Wright was profoundly affected by Emerson's belief that only the individual, through the discipline of principles learned from experience, could effect the integration of culture and nature that was the promise of America. Emerson also held that one should concentrate on one's own insights, intuitions and abilities: 'Insist on yourself; never imitate. Your own gift you can present every moment with the cumulative force of a whole life's cultivation.' Wright's often combative stance in his dealings with later criticism can be traced directly to Emerson: 'Whoever would be a man, must be a nonconformist'; 'Nothing is at last sacred but the integrity of your own mind'; and, most tellingly, 'To be great is to be misunderstood.'

Yet, as developed in Emerson's writings, this emphasis on the individual experience was optimistic, encouraging each of us to search history for the fundamental principles of human existence, to look beyond the failings of contemporary society to find the essential and unchanging nature of man. Emerson's fellow traveller Thoreau noted, 'The improvements of the ages have but little influence on the essential laws of man's existence.'[19] Emerson's writings, and the Transcendentalist tradition, focused on the value of each individual's experience, and in his own work Wright would place the greatest emphasis on the inhabitant's experience of the space within. The cumulative effect of Emerson's thought in Wright's architecture has been characterized as its emphasis 'on the celebration of everyday life', on integrating with the natural world around us, and on the 'enrichment of experience'.[20]

The patriarch of the Valley, Wright's grandfather Richard Lloyd Jones, died in early 1886 and his unmarried daughters, Wright's

aunts Nell and Jane, inherited the farm and homestead. That same
year they established the Hillside Home School, using the newly
opened Unity Chapel as their temporary classroom. Unity Chapel,
which seated 200 worshippers, had been finished in summer 1886
to the designs of the Chicago architect Joseph Lyman Silsbee, who
was simultaneously designing the new All Souls Church in Chicago
for Jenkin Lloyd Jones. Wright had also made a design for the new
chapel; when his uncle chose instead to employ Silsbee, Wright
was allowed to help oversee construction of Unity Chapel. Wright
would claim in later years that various aspects of the interior of
Unity Chapel, including the square red and green ceiling panels,
were of his design.

In January 1886, following his father's departure, the eighteen-
year-old Wright had enrolled as a special student at the University
of Wisconsin; over the next two semesters he took courses in
French, English composition, mathematics and engineering. He
also worked part-time for a professor of engineering, Allan D.
Conover, in his private practice in downtown Madison. The office
was at this time involved in supervising the building of the new
Science Hall on campus, so this, along with the Unity Chapel,
provided Wright with his first experiences in construction. Wright
recalls reading voraciously during his time at the University, as well
as taking classes in stereotomy (projection of three-dimensional
solids, used to shape stones), graphic statics of structures, and
analytical and descriptive geometry – all involving drawing – with
Professors Conover and Storm Bull, whose name indicates his
native American heritage.

It was during this period that Wright witnessed an architectural
tragedy when the new north wing of the State Capitol in Madison,
then under construction, collapsed and killed a number of workers.
Wright recalled seeing people buried as the interior floors and
columns fell, leaving only the outer walls standing, and a worker
who was pinned to the side of the building, causing 'a ghastly red

stream' to run down the stone wall. The effect on Wright was long-lasting, the cause of subsequent nightmares, and some 45 years later he wrote of his own reaction (in the third person): 'The horror of the scene has never entirely left his consciousness, and remains to prompt him to this day.'[21]

While he later claimed that he was enrolled in the University of Wisconsin through the middle of his senior, or fourth year, in fact Wright decided to leave Madison for Chicago in early 1887, aged nineteen. This was against his mother's wishes and his uncle Jenkin's advice; when Anna wrote to her brother, at All Souls Church, he responded, 'On no account let the young man come to Chicago. He should stay in Madison and finish his education. That will do more good for him than anything else. If he comes here he can only waste himself on fine clothes and girls.'[22] Wright found the letter insulting, and only a few days later, having sold his father's copies of Plutarch's *Parallel Lives* (his favourite) and Gibbon's *The History of the Decline and Fall of the Roman Empire* (which he says he despised), as well as a mink collar his mother had sewn into one of his coats, he left, taking the Northwestern train to Chicago, which he called 'the Eternal City of the West'.[23]

2

Chicago and the Tradition of Practice 1887–93

Chicago. Wells Street Station: six o'clock in late spring, 1887. Drizzling. Sputtering white arc-light in the station and on the streets, dazzling and ugly. I had never seen electric lights before. Crowds. Impersonal, intent on seeing nothing . . . So cold, black, blue-white, and wet. The horrid blue-white glare of arc-lights was over everything . . . A Chicago murderously actual . . . Immense gridiron of noisy streets. Dirty . . . Terrible, this grinding and piling up of blind forces. If there was a logic here who could grasp it?

This grim litany of ugliness and chaos is the way Wright would remember his arrival in Chicago in writing his autobiography more than 40 years later. Yet, wandering through the city that first night, he happened to stop on one of the swing-bridges as it opened to allow a tug pushing a grain boat to pass, and Wright was 'charmed by [the] somber beauty' of the Chicago River.[1] Later he bought a ticket to a musical comedy at the Grand Opera House, the interior of which had been built in 1880 to the designs of the architectural firm of Dankmar Adler, with young Louis Sullivan the designer.[2]

Wright spent his second, third and fourth day in the city searching for work among the architects building the new Chicago that was now rising phoenix-like from the ashes of the Great Fire, which had consumed the majority of the city in one day on 9 April 1871. The new construction, necessary to accommodate the doubling of the city's population that had occurred in the single decade of 1880–90, had only been able to begin in earnest at the end of the extended economic depression of the previous decade.

In the Pullman Building, Wright visited the office of its architect, Solon Beman, who was also employed by railroad magnate George Pullman as the designer of his new town of Pullman outside Chicago, where thousands of workers who made Pullman Train Cars both lived and laboured. On his way to the office of W. W. Boyington, Wright passed by the Chicago Board of Trade Building, an eclectic mish-mash of many historical styles, and his reaction was immediate; 'Boyington had done it. This? – thin-chested, hard-faced, chamfered monstrosity? I turned aside from Boyington's office then and there.'[3]

Wright next went to the office of William Le Baron Jenney, who two years before had built the first iron-framed structure in Chicago, the Home Insurance Company. Jenney was the only classically trained architect and engineer in Chicago when he arrived there following the Civil War. During the war he had been a member of General William Tecumseh Sherman's corps of engineers, whose efforts, including the development of interchangeable truss sections that allowed the Union bridges to be rebuilt as fast as the Southern forces could destroy them, made it possible for Sherman to move large numbers of men and equipment at lightning speed through rough terrain, bringing the Civil War to an early end.[4] Jenney was the first architect to ask Wright if he had any drawings to show him, telling him to bring them to the next meeting of the Chicago Architectural Club, of which Jenney was at that time president.

Wright wrote that he visited eight more offices, all without success, until at last he decided to go to the office of Joseph Lyman Silsbee, architect for Unity Chapel in the Valley and his uncle Jenkin Lloyd Jones's All Souls Church in Chicago. While having his first meal in Chicago, which cost him ten per cent of his savings of seven dollars, Wright had vowed not to ask his uncle Jenkin for help, nor to use his name or connections. Yet it is very doubtful that Wright, who had assisted the Silsbee office with the interior design of the Unity Chapel the previous spring, would not have been recognized by either Silsbee or someone else in the office, as he later claimed. It is far more likely that Silsbee notified Jenkin Lloyd Jones of his nephew's application for work at his office, and received the influential clergyman and repeat client's blessing. Wright was hired to start at eight dollars a week, and the next week his uncle found him a boarding room nearby. This would be the first of many instances where Jenkin Lloyd Jones would positively influence the young architect's career.

Silsbee had a penchant for hiring young talent, and in his office during the time Wright was employed were George Maher and George Elmslie, who would go on to become important Prairie School architects, and Cecil Corwin, another minister's son, who became one of Wright's closest friends and later his associate in practice. In turn, it was Silsbee's talent for drawing that first attracted and astonished Wright: on seeing the architect's sketches pinned to the walls when he came to interview, Silsbee's pencil strokes 'like standing corn in the field waving in the breeze', Wright immediately 'liked the atmosphere of the office'.[5] This was an entirely natural reaction for someone both talented in drawing and trained in the Froebel methods, since, according to Froebel, 'it is in drawing that the child pre-eminently shows himself to be creative.'[6]

In his designs Silsbee was influenced by the wood shingle-clad houses of Henry Hobson Richardson, considered the father of American architecture by his contemporaries. This architecture's picturesque, horizontally banded massing was a direct expression of the formal flexibility of the wooden shingles with which the walls and roofs were covered, as exemplified in Silsbee's little Unity Chapel, a perspective drawing of which Wright made for publication soon after joining the firm. Wright recalled his employer's design process: 'Silsbee got a ground-plan and made his pretty

Portrait of Wright, left, and his friend and later business associate Cecil Corwin, right, *c.* 1888.

sketch, getting some charming picturesque effect he had in his mind. Then the sketch would come out into the draughting room to be fixed up into a building, keeping the floor-plan near the sketch if possible.' Corwin noted, 'The picture interests him. The rest bores him.'[7]

Wright would later reject this use of the perspective sketch as the starting point of design, instead using the perspective as a final 'proof' or test of a design, an idea found in Viollet-le-Duc's *Discourses on Architecture,* which Wright read in Madison, and representing in Wright's work 'a rare marriage between an abstract system of design and the requirements of the eye'.[8] Although he arrived at this insight by way of reaction against Silsbee's design methods, Wright also wrote that during his year in Silsbee's office he 'gained considerable light on the practical needs of the American dwelling', and that he 'learned a good deal about a house from Silsbee by way of Cecil'.[9]

During his later months at Silsbee's, Wright and Corwin were inseparable. In a period photograph of the two young architects, Wright, his fine coat open to reveal his waistcoat and stiff collar, is facing the camera, while Corwin, seen in profile, his hand on Wright's shoulder, is looking not at the camera but at Wright. Wright's wavy hair, which he wore long when he arrived from Madison (where his nickname was 'Shaggy'), is at this time cut fashionably short. After work Wright and Corwin would dine out, at the local Italian restaurant if they were not flush with money, at the Tip-Top Inn at the Pullman Building if they were.

At this time the famous conductor Theodore Thomas, then with the New York Philharmonic Orchestra, who had for twenty years been giving concerts throughout the United States to rave reviews, was playing in the Chicago Opera Festival Auditorium, inside the massive Inter-State Industrial Exposition Building on the lakefront. In 1885 this building had been renovated and made acoustically resonant 'to the faintest pianissimo' by Adler and Sullivan.[10] Wright recalled that in the rear of the auditorium 'were tables and refreshments in comfortable German style. I've never enjoyed any concerts more since.'[11]

The success of these Chicago concerts by Thomas and his touring orchestra had the previous year convinced their sponsor, Ferdinand Peck, descendant of one of the city's founders, that the time had arrived for Chicago to build its own permanent concert hall to rival the Metropolitan Opera House in New York. This, coupled with the desire by Chicago's powerful business leaders in the Commercial Club to lure Thomas to Chicago from New York, had led to the commissioning of the Auditorium Building, the largest architectural project in the history of the city. The project had been widely expected to go to the premier architectural firm in the city, that of Daniel Hudson Burnham and John Wellborn Root. The job went instead, however, to the much smaller and less well-known firm of Adler and Sullivan, 'because it was Peck's project and he considered Adler to be the best acoustical engineer and theater designer in the country'.[12]

Yet it would be Sullivan whose reputation as a leading designer would be established by the Auditorium Building. Under construction starting in early 1887, almost the exact moment Wright arrived in Chicago, the Auditorium has been said to be 'as important a build-ing for nineteenth-century Chicago as Brunelleschi's cathedral cupola had been for fifteenth-century Florence, and like that stupendous dome, it was an engineering as well as an artistic challenge.'[13] The mammoth Auditorium Building, at the corner of Congress Street and Michigan Avenue, facing Lake Michigan, was a multi-use building housing a 4,300-seat opera theatre and a 400-room luxury hotel, as well as extensive commercial offices, all topped by a tower, the rooftop observatory of which would be the highest point in the city when the building was completed.

Watching this great building under construction, its innovative cantilevered steel-frame foundations developed by Adler to bear in Chicago's notoriously muddy soil, Wright was soon drawn to the firm of Adler and Sullivan. After spending three days and nights making drawings to prove his abilities to depict Sullivan's complex ornament, 'like the passion vine – in full bloom',[14] in 1888 Wright left Silsbee, where he was making eighteen dollars a week, to work with Sullivan, being paid $25 a week and working in the firm's top-floor offices in Adler's Borden Block. Wright initially was set to work on drawings for the Auditorium interiors, and soon he was deeply involved in every aspect of the great building's ornamental, functional and acoustical design, as well as its innovative structure and construction, an apprenticeship in practice unparalleled any-where in the world at that time.

Louis Sullivan, the son of Irish immigrants, had grown up in Boston, where he saw several of Richardson's most accomplished works being built, and entered the Massachusetts Institute of Technology when he was sixteen. He left the school before complet-ing his studies, however, moving to Philadelphia to work briefly for Frank Furness, but he was let go due to the economic downturn of the 1870s. At age seventeen Sullivan was drawn to the great rebuilding, and redefinition of modern construction, taking place in Chicago. In 1873 he was employed in Jenney's office, and there met John Edelmann, Jenney's young foreman, who introduced Sullivan to German philosophy and the music of Richard Wagner.[15]

After a year in Jenney's office Sullivan left to attend the Ecole des Beaux-Arts in Paris. But he again became bored with academic instruction and during a trip to Rome, sitting alone for hours in the Sistine Chapel, he came to realize that, as Emerson had said, imitation was not the path to true beauty. Returning to Chicago, Sullivan could not find steady employment during the depression, and studied engineering on his own, particularly the works of the great American bridge builders. In 1880 he joined Adler's firm as chief designer, becoming a full partner three years later at age 27. This remarkable early success was in fact entirely the norm in Chicago, where in 1880 the average age of Chicago architects was under thirty.[16] When Wright joined the firm of Adler and Sullivan in 1888 as a designer at age 21, Sullivan was only eleven years his senior.

Sullivan was not only a designer of rare talent, he was also full of what were then called 'large ideas, tending to metaphysics'.[17] Sullivan was as much an inheritor of the Transcendentalist tradition as Wright, and was also by this time deeply involved in natural geometries. Sullivan, like the Transcendentalists, was influenced by the writings of Horatio Greenough (1805–1852), an American sculptor and essayist who lived in Rome for much of his life. Greenough wrote with particular passion on modern architecture's relation to historical form, holding that to draw from history one must 'learn principles, not copy shapes'.[18] Before 1850 he had already articulated the principle that 'form follows function', and held that 'the edifices in whose construction the principles of architecture are developed may be classed as organic.' Paralleling his contemporary Froebel, Greenough called for the close study of nature and development of forms from an inner conception: 'Instead of forcing the functions of every sort of building into one general form, adapting an outward shape for the sake of the eye or of association, without reference to the inner distribution, let us begin from the heart as the nucleus, and work outwards.'

This concept of developing architecture from an inner core ('seed-germ'), which is then unfurled like a flower, was critical to Sullivan's philosophy and to his efforts to remedy Greenough's stinging charge:

> The mind of this country has never been seriously applied to the subject of building. Intently engaged in matters of more pressing importance, we have been content to receive our notions of architecture as we have received the fashion of our garments and the forms of our entertainments, from Europe.[19]

Sullivan keenly felt the absence of a true American architecture, yet in 1885 he had warned against efforts to speed its arrival by 'transplanting and grafting' historical styles onto the American continent. He believed, as had Emerson, that any true indigenous American architecture would develop on a regional basis, with variations dependent upon climate, landscape and local building methods.[20]

Having experienced it himself, Sullivan was sceptical as to whether contemporary architectural education in the United States, based as it was on academic exercises in the predetermined classical style, would ever allow the development of forms that followed function, much less an appropriate American architecture. He believed instead that architectural education, starting well before college, should cultivate what he called the 'common sense' of analytical thinking, and his 1901 essays on the subject were titled, significantly enough, *Kindergarten Chats*.

In his own work, Sullivan built from his belief that nature could be the source for geometric form in architecture, developed as a dialogue between Chicago's great discovery, the structural frame, and its ornamented cladding. While later historians have often focused on the striving to achieve ever more height evident in the early development of the Chicago skyscraper, it was in fact initially the need to provide interior spaces with ever more natural light that drove Jenney and the other early pioneers. In this, the thin structural frame, initially made of iron, and soon after steel, was essential. Yet Sullivan believed that the manner in which the steel frame was clad, and the humanizing of the static structure through integral ornament – *of* the surface, rather than *on* it – is what was required to transform the Chicago frame skyscraper into a true work of architecture.

Sullivan's theory of ornament, which he was developing at the time Wright was in his office, was, like the Froebel training, both a philosophy and a method of formal composition. The year he entered the office of Adler and Sullivan, Wright had found in the library of All Souls Church a copy of Owen Jones's *The Grammar of Ornament* (London, 1856). In their after-hours talks over the next five years Sullivan and Wright carefully studied this extraordinary book, with its hundreds of colour plates of ornamental patterns from around the world, discerning the ancient geometries that structured and united them. The fact that Jones, Sullivan and Wright were all of Celtic extraction only reinforced the two architects' interest in ornamental examples from outside what they considered to be the endlessly imitated and exhausted Western tradition of Greece and Rome. Of particular interest were Celtic patterns, which Jones's book stated were brought to Ireland from the East, and Islamic patterns originating in the geometric figures of the square, hexagon, octagon and dodecahedron.

Sullivan and Wright enjoyed a particularly close intellectual relationship, unlike any Wright would ever again share with another architect, and Sullivan's challenges became Wright's own. Trained in architecture, not in an academic setting but through the tradition of practice, similar to a medieval guild apprenticeship, Wright became, as he said, 'a good pencil in the Master's hand',[21] his talent freeing Sullivan to engage ever-larger philosophical agendas in his lecturing and writing. It was during this time that Sullivan was corresponding with Walt Whitman, the great American poet and author of *Leaves of Grass*, originally written in 1855, which he was then rewriting for new publication in 1891/2. Sullivan believed his designs and thinking were actively engaging the same philosophical conceptions underlying the works of Emerson and Whitman, and that in his own ornament, which he understood to be a fusion of nature and culture, lay the key to an appropriate American architecture.

Other than his *Lieber Meister* ('beloved master'), as he called Sullivan, the only people Wright became close to in the office were Paul Mueller, a young engineer from Stuttgart who would later build many of Wright's great buildings, and Dankmar Adler, the senior partner and brilliant engineer. Adler, who had also been part of General Sherman's famous engineering corps in the Civil War, would later be credited by Wright as introducing the ideal of 'form follows function' into the work of the office – not Sullivan, with whom the phrase is most often associated, due to Sullivan's use of it in many speeches. Adler's approach to structural engineering was innovative and experimental, and this had a strong influence on Wright's understanding of structures, reinforcing both the cautionary experience of the collapse of the State Capitol at Madison and his childhood experiences building with his uncle Thomas. From Adler Wright also learned about the nascent science of acoustics, reinforcing the great importance of music in his life, as well as the hours he spent listening to his father play the organ and piano in various spaces. As a result of his close study with Adler, in later years Wright's exceptional skills in both structures and acoustics seemed almost intuitive.

It was through Adler, the son of a prominent rabbi, that the firm received many of its commissions from the German-Jewish community of Chicago. During the last quarter of the nineteenth century

German culture exercised enormous influence over Chicago, with a full one-third of the city's population of one million in 1890 being German immigrants and speakers. The city had two German-language daily papers, and Adler and Sullivan's Auditorium was constructed to house Wagner operas, as their 1892 Schiller Theater was commissioned to house plays performed in German.

At exactly the time Wright was working for Adler and Sullivan, the architectural theories of German architect and teacher Gottfried Semper were being introduced to Chicago by the German émigré Frederick Bauman and the American John Root, partner of Burnham. Bauman, who developed a new method of constructing building foundations, presented Semper's ideas in lectures given to Chicago's architects in 1887, 1890 and 1892. Root, married to the sister of Harriet Monroe, the poet who would found the magazine *Poetry* in 1912, was an exceptionally talented designer, one of only two contemporary architects Sullivan respected, along with H. H. Richardson. In 1889 and 1890 Root published translations he had made with German émigré Fritz Wagner, a specialist in terracotta facing of the kind both Root and Sullivan were then employing to clad steel frames, of Semper's 1869 treatise *Über Baustile*.[22]

The aspect of Semper's theories that would have resonated with Sullivan and Wright was his understanding that the origin of all built form lay in textile production – in weaving. This led directly to Semper's theory of cladding, wherein the screen-like walls of architecture, particularly facings of terracotta ('baked earth'), masonry and brickwork, were conceived as a woven fabric dressing the structural frame beneath. Using as his model the Caribbean hut, from the New World island of Trinidad, which he had seen in London in the Crystal Palace at the Great Exhibition of 1851, Semper argued that primordial building was enacted in a series of four distinct stages: first, marking the ground and constructing the foundation; second, making the hearth; third, erecting the structural frame; and fourth, cladding the frame with a woven fabric to enclose the walls and roof. Finally, Semper believed – as did Sullivan and Wright – that architecture, as a rhythmic weaving of space and material, was far closer in nature to poetic chants, music and dance than to either painting or sculpture.[23]

This conception of weaving as a way of understanding the making of architecture is reflected in the differences between Sullivan and Wright's architecture and that of their Beaux-Arts trained contemporaries: differences not only between their formal languages, but, far more importantly, between the nature of their processes of design. It has recently been noted that the method taught at the Ecole des Beaux-Arts was in fact not a design process at all, but rather a predetermined compositional procedure, an 'art of command' where the architect dictates the form of the building, based upon preconceived precedents, and the materials out of which it is made have no effect on the design. On the other hand, Sullivan and Wright practised the 'art of nurture', a process of design where the architect seeks a fit between function and form, fitting the spatial geometry to the pattern of human activity, and where the nature of the materials with which the design is made has a significant effect on the design.[24] In this description, as in the Froebel training, weaving metaphors abound, as they would in Wright's later description of his own design process.

In early 1888, at the time Wright secured a position at Adler and Sullivan, construction was already underway on the Hillside Home School in the Valley, the first of what became a steady stream of 'moonlight' commissions Wright would take on over the next five years to support his always escalating expenses. Wright had designed this entirely shingle-clad, house-like structure, where students would both live and attend classes, for his schoolteacher aunts Jane and Nell the year before, while working at Silsbee's office. The design of this, Wright's first realized work, was clearly influenced by Silsbee's formal language, as well as his tendency to give institutional buildings a residential character, as exemplified by Jenkin Lloyd Jones's All Souls Church.

At this same time Wright also met sixteen-year-old Catherine Tobin at a study class on Victor Hugo's *Les Misérables* at All Souls Church, led by his uncle Jenkin. Actually, Wright recalls running headlong into Kitty, as her parents called her, during a dance at a costume party marking the end of the study class. After Wright had helped her back to her feet, her parents invited him to their house for dinner the next night, and Wright remembers walking home alone, enchanted – he was in love. Catherine, a member of one of the wealthier families in Jones's congregation, was clearly equally smitten with Wright, the nephew of the famous minister and social leader. Catherine was her parents' only daughter, their pride and joy, as Wright was his mother's favourite, and up to this time they had both led fairly sheltered existences. Their romance developed rapidly, opposed by both his and her parents.

Wright's mother and youngest sister Maginel came to live with him at this time, and the family decided to settle in Oak Park, a new suburb a few miles west of downtown Chicago. For the first year they lived as boarders in a redbrick house on Forest Avenue, owned and occupied by Augusta Chapin, a friend of Anna Wright's and the pastor of the Oak Park Universalist Church. Despite the best efforts of both their parents, including Catherine's parents sending her away for three months and Wright's mother's often devious attempts to dissuade first him, then her, the young couple were determined to marry when Catherine turned eighteen. On 1 June 1889, as it poured rain outside, they were married. During the ceremony Catherine's father, Samuel Tobin, burst into tears and Anna Wright fainted.

In Oak Park, near Revd Chapin's house, Wright found the building site for his house, fronting on Forest Avenue at the corner of Chicago Avenue, with a small cottage adjacent for his mother and two sisters. Anna agreed to sell her Madison house, but in order to buy the property and build the house Wright needed more money. Having now worked for Adler and Sullivan for a year, in 1889 he approached Adler, who agreed to a five-year contract at $60 a week (making Wright the highest paid draughtsman in Chicago), and Sullivan, who offered a loan of $5,000, to be repaid in weekly instalments from Wright's pay. After the purchase of the lot, Wright had $3,500 remaining to build the house, but he went $1,200 over this budget, a fact he hid from Sullivan.

Oak Park, also known as 'Saints' Rest' because of its many churches, was a rapidly growing suburb of Chicago. The term 'suburb' had not yet been coined and Wright referred to Oak Park as a village, remembering both its generously shaded streets and its 'miles of expensive mummery'; rows of uninspired wooden houses, each with a front porch 'squirming with wanton scroll-work' and a 'murderous corner-tower' topped by a 'candle-snuffer roof'.[25] But Oak Park was also being inhabited by wealthy and progressive families moving from the city to escape the chaotic lack of planning and poor quality of construction for which Chicago was by this time rightly infamous. Oak Park, later the birthplace of novelist Ernest Hemingway, would serve as the perfect place for Wright to establish himself as an architect and, in retrospect, his choice at age 22 of this quiet village as his home appears remarkably prescient.

Wright's modest little house in Oak Park is full of suggestive details and spatial implications, and we can safely assume that it was intended to exemplify Wright's emerging architectural ideals. The massing of the front of the house, as seen from Forest Avenue, is deceptively simple yet memorable, with an enormous pyramidal gable, sheathed entirely in wood shingles, floating over a recessed entry floor, its glazed windows weaving in and out of the shadow, the whole raised on a stone plinth and protected by a terrace wall.

The plan for the house was based directly on the then-standard builder's prototype, called the 'four-square' because of its four basic spaces on the main, lower floor (entry/stair, living room, dining

Sitting on the porch of Oak Park house are Catherine Wright with infant, Anna Lloyd Jones (behind Catherine) and the architect (to the right).

room and kitchen), all held within a square plan anchored at the centre by the hearth and its inglenook. While the exterior is closed and solid in appearance, inside Wright removed large parts of the walls normally separating the three main rooms in the first inkling of what would later be known as the open plan. Using bands of wood trim that run continuously around each room at door-top height, Wright constructed boundaries that are closed above, at the ceiling, and open below, at the floor. In their daily rituals of domestic life, the movements of his family between rooms, spiralling around the fireplace at the centre, wove together the spaces of the house in a manner unlike any other Western architecture of the time.

Yet many elements in the interior of Wright's Oak Park house are ordered in a manner strikingly similar to those found in traditional Japanese domestic architecture, including the wrapping wood trim band at door-top height and the domestic 'altar' (hearth) at the centre. While Wright's first exposure to Japanese architecture would not occur until four years later, he was clearly already quite familiar with the traditional Japanese house, and used it as a starting point in designing his own house. Wright evidently had read contemporary publications on Far Eastern art and culture, then fashionable in both America and Britain, yet it was far more important that the world's leading authority on traditional Japanese culture, Ernesto Fenollosa, was Silsbee's first cousin, giving Wright a direct connection to the most recent scholarship.[26]

At Adler and Sullivan, Wright's talent was recognized from the start, and after the firm moved into the top floor of the tower of the newly completed Auditorium Building, he was given a private office opening directly to Sullivan's room. Besides the Auditorium itself, Wright was involved in the designs of some of the firm's greatest buildings, including the Pueblo Opera House, Colorado; the Dooly Commercial Block; the Tomb for Carrie Getty; the Wainwright Building in St Louis; the Schiller Theater and Office Building; the Transportation Building for the World's Columbian Exposition; the unbuilt Odd Fellows Temple; the Brunswick Balke Factory; the Mayer Warehouse; the Tomb for Charlotte Wainwright in St Louis; the St Nicholas and Victoria Hotels; the Union Trust Building; and the beginning of the Chicago Stock Exchange Building.

In addition to his full-time day job, Wright took home evening or 'moonlight' projects. As he recalled, 'Adler and Sullivan refused to build residences during all the period I was with them. The few that were imperative owing to social obligations to important clients fell to my lot out of office hours.'[27] Wright was thus primarily responsible for the designs of the vacation cottages in Ocean Springs, Mississippi, for the Charnley family and Sullivan himself; the townhouse for Sullivan's mother; and the James Charnley House of 1891, built on Astor Place in Chicago.

One of the greatest works of architecture of the period, the Charnley House surpassed the similar urban houses of Wright's

mature contemporaries, such as the firm he called Richardson's
'elite running competition', McKim, Mead and White of New York,
and is an absolutely astonishing work for an architect of 24. It was
in the design of the Charnley House façade that Wright recalls he
'first sensed the definitely decorative value of the plain surface . . .
the flat plane,'[28] an idea likely inspired by a lecture given by John
Root to young Chicago architects in 1887, in which Root stated:
'The value of plain surfaces in every building is not to be overesti-
mated. Strive for them . . .'.[29]

Wright cites the 'other debts pressing' him, including the support
of his children, Frank Jr (called Lloyd), John and Catherine, all born
by 1893, and his mother and sisters, as the reason that, starting in
1890, he took on other 'bootleg' house designs, as he called them,
in addition to the office's 'moonlight' residential work. These include
the houses built for the families of Dr Allison Harlan, George
Blossom, Warren MacArthur, Robert Parker, Thomas Gale and
Robert Emmond. These houses, although designed by Wright, were
announced in building industry publications as being the work of
his close friend Cecil Corwin, who had recently left Silsbee's office.

All of these houses share a relatively understated, quiet appearance on the exterior, complemented by the often highly innovative
and dynamic organization of their interior spaces. Examples include
the cruciform plan of the Blossom House, precursor to Wright's
ideal plan form in later years, and the MacArthur House fireplace,
which stands between the two main rooms with open passages on
either side, exactly as would occur sixteen years later in the Robie
House. Here we see the first instances of what would become a
life-long pattern: Wright developed his revolutionary spatial
conceptions first in interior spaces, only later arriving at an appropriate mode of expressing these spaces on the exterior – working
from the inside outwards.

Despite his later claims of never having been influenced by
contemporary architects, and historians of modern architecture

holding that he was an 'inventor' of entirely unprecedented 'new' forms, in fact Wright's process of design was dependent upon the work of others. Writing about this early period of independent work, Wright was quite direct about this: 'I could not invent terms of my own overnight.'[30] Wright's design process for these houses involved taking as a starting point a design by an older, widely recognized contemporary (often McKim, Mead and White), which he then improved and perfected so that in the end his own design far surpassed its 'model' in both quality and resolution, as if to show them all how it should be done.

Almost 40 years later Wright wrote that in early 1893 Sullivan discovered his 'bootleg' houses; after a brief but bitter argument, and an attempt at intervention by Adler, Wright threw down his pencil and walked out of the office. Recent research has suggested that Sullivan must have known about Wright's personal projects at least a year before their confrontation, as Sullivan and his brother were both living in close proximity to the Harlan, Blossom and MacArthur Houses, and it is hardly possible that Sullivan failed to take note of these distinctive designs as they were being constructed.[31] There is perhaps more to this story, but Wright's break with Sullivan was deep and painfully serious, and they would remain at a distance for fifteen years.

3

White City and New World Monumentality 1893–99

After five years with Adler and Sullivan, Wright opened his own office in 1893, sharing space in the eighteenth or top floor of the Schiller Building tower (a space remarkably similar to Sullivan's office at the top of the Auditorium tower) with Corwin, his old friend from Silsbee's office and architect of record for the 'bootleg' houses. The Schiller Building of 1891, which houses a theatre, a social club and offices, with an observation platform on the roof of the tower, owed more to Wright's design than was usual at Adler and Sullivan. As Wright wrote, 'the Schiller Building, Chicago – a building owing to Sullivan's love for his new home in the South [Ocean Springs, Mississippi – designed by Wright], more largely left to me than any other so far.'[1]

In his own work Wright continued to explore the two primary 'missions' underlying both his daytime and 'moonlight' work at Adler and Sullivan: the search for an appropriate form of monumentality through the evolution of new building types; and the development of a regionally inflected model for the new, 'reformed' single-family home – at that time the most pressing challenges for the Chicago architects attempting to find an American way of building.

Wright's first client in his new office was William H. Winslow, president of the Winslow Ornamental Iron Works, who commissioned a house in River Forest, a Chicago suburb adjacent to Oak Park. In many ways Winslow was typical of the clients who would come to Wright over the next two decades: almost all were businessmen, often self-employed, many involved in manufacturing or industry (often as inventors), who felt their making useful things to be far more important than their simply making money. They involved music and art in their home life and supported both in their public life; they were economically conservative, generally voting Republican, yet were disinterested in emulating the conventional houses of the city's commercial leaders; and they all shared a strong support of women's suffrage.[2] This combination of characteristics in his clients often led to Wright engaging in avocational collaborations with them, such as Revd W. C. Gannett's book *The House Beautiful*, with its intricately ornamented pages designed by Wright, which was printed on Winslow's basement press in 1896.

The plan of the Winslow House is a further evolution of the plan of Wright's own house in Oak Park, with a magnificently detailed fireplace and inglenook anchoring the centre, around which the library, entry hall, living room and dining room rotate, the spatial sequence culminating in the semi-circular dining room bay projecting to the rear of the house, with its continuous band of leaded glass windows. While the house has received appropriate attention as the first of Wright's independent works, the stables (later garage) behind the house is where Wright first explored an early version of both the plan and elevation languages of the Prairie House. Not being under the same requirements for formality as the main house, the stables undoubtedly offered Wright a greater opportunity for experimentation.

The front elevation of the Winslow House, with its smooth brick base rising to the sill of the first-floor windows, which are contained in a continuous horizontal band of ornamented terracotta tiles, and the broad overhanging roof above, is clearly a precursor to the fully evolved Prairie House. Yet it is also remarkably similar to a recently completed building with which Wright would have been familiar, the Turkish National Pavilion at the World's Columbian Exposition, which opened in Chicago that same year.

In the last quarter of the nineteenth century a struggle for influence had developed between 'indigenous' American architecture, exemplified by the Chicago skyscraper and the evolution of regional models for the middle-class single-family house, and 'universal' academic classical architecture, exemplified by the work of Ecole des Beaux-Arts trained architects, based largely in New York and Boston. A primary issue in this struggle was the appropriate form of monumentality for the American nation, only then emerging as a new world power. The balance between these two schools of thought was dramatically changed by the World's Columbian Exposition, which was awarded to Chicago, after a heated competition with New York, in 1890.

The first designer selected to work on the Exposition was Frederick Law Olmstead, America's greatest landscape architect, and though 'remembered best in history as a spectacular architectural show, the Columbian Exposition's most impressive design accomplishment was actually Olmstead and [Burnham's partner] Root's artful reshaping of an unsightly split of sand and swamp water' along the shore of Lake Michigan into Jackson Park, one of the most beautiful urban landscapes in America.[3]

Daniel Burnham was appointed director of the works and, in what was immediately perceived as a blow to the Chicago School of architecture, Burnham chose only Beaux-Arts trained easterners as the architects for the principal buildings: Richard Hunt, founder and president of the American Institute of Architects, McKim, George Post, Henry Van Brunt, and the partnership of Robert Peabody and John Stearns. Responding to the uproar in Chicago, particularly among the captains of industry who were the Exposition's primary sponsors, Burnham added Beman (Pullman's architect), Jenney, and Adler and Sullivan to the group. Yet even with this adjustment, made largely in response to local political pressures, the Exposition was widely seen as a clear indication that the influence of the Chicago School of architecture (and Sullivan in particular) was on the wane.

Seeming to sense this, Sullivan's participation (as 'Secretary') in the Exposition architects' planning meetings consisted of long periods of silence punctuated by pointedly sarcastic comments. In the end Sullivan was given the Transportation Building to design, on a site well removed from the Court of Honor, the Italian Renaissance-style centrepiece of the Columbian Exposition and the inspiration for its name, the White City.

By 1886, the year before Wright arrived, Chicago had become the centre of radicalism, anarchism and trade unionism in America. That same year Chicago was the site of the Haymarket Riots, when marching workers clashed with the police and military units protecting the city's commercial interests, and during which a bomb was thrown among the police, who responded with random gunfire. The Columbian Exposition was in many ways a response to this tragedy, and 'it was hardly coincidental that the city that staged, in 1893, the century's most impressive demonstration of civic order was the one that was shaken by the century's most terrifying single outburst of urban disorder.'[4]

The story of the construction of the Columbian Exposition is an extraordinary one, and it simply would not have happened without the almost superhuman efforts of Burnham, who willed the White City into being in twenty months, this despite a string of cata-strophic setbacks, any one of which would have defeated most men. The first and most devastating of these occurred when Burnham's partner, Chicago's leading designer and theoretician John Root, died of pneumonia at age 40, before the planning of the Exposition had even started. In constructing the Exposition on its 685-acre site, more than one million plants, shrubs and trees were planted, 36,000 freight-car loads of materials were brought in on dedicated rail lines to build more than 200 individual structures, including some of the largest in the world at the time, and many hundreds of workers were employed – among them was the father of Walt Disney.[5]

During the Exposition's construction, Chicago saw a building boom like none before, including the construction of the Art Institute, which was soon drawing more visitors annually than any other American museum, and the first buildings of the newly established University of Chicago, which rapidly became one of the most esteemed institutions of its kind in the nation. Thousands of young people moved to Chicago to work on the White City itself, or on the hundreds of other new buildings rising rapidly all over the city, as well as those who came seeking employment in the businesses serving attendees of the Exposition. In the year after its opening in 1893 the Exposition drew 27 million visitors, 14 million of them from outside the US, 'making it the greatest tourist attraction in American history'.[6]

Taking advantage of this extraordinary influx of people to the city, many parallel events were held, including the World Parliament of Religions of September 1893, a gathering of more than a hundred religious leaders from every faith around the world, whose twice-a-day lectures and discussions were attended by audiences of 4,000 – all organized by Wright's uncle Jenkin Lloyd Jones, author that same year of the book *Religions of the World*. The World Congress of Historians brought University of Wisconsin professor and later progressive leader Frederick Jackson Turner to the White City, where he lectured on 'The Significance of the Frontier in American History', saying that the frontier has been the source of 'individualism', 'self-reliance' and 'inventiveness', and that American democracy 'came out of the forest, and it gained strength each time it touched a new frontier' – ideas that would have the greatest import for Wright.[7]

Also among those who came to Chicago during this period was a man who called himself H. H. Holmes, the first urban mass murderer in America, who built a house of horror called 'the castle' at 63rd and Wallace Streets in Englewood, where he is alleged to have killed as many as 100 people before, during and after the

Exposition, most of them young women who came to the city in search of a better life.[8]

During his visits to the White City Wright was able to carefully study the Japanese Pavilion, the 'Ho-o-den', or Phoenix Hall, the main central pavilion of which was based on the Ho-o-do Temple at the Byodo-in, Uji, near Kyoto, while the interiors and outer wings were modelled on traditional Japanese aristocratic houses. The drawings for the structure had been published in Chicago's *Inland Architect* in December 1892, and it was constructed by traditionally trained wood craftsmen brought from Japan, a process documented in the newspapers and open to the public, 10,000 of whom visited the Exposition each day during its construction. Wright, as one of the architects working on the Transportation Building, had access to the White City's construction site from the start.

The effect on Wright of the 'Ho-o-den' was immediate, and in his work he took as his own and transformed numerous of its aspects, including the cruciform plan; the horizontal proportions; the screen-like walls that slid open and closed under the continuous wrapping door-top beam; the lack of rigid interior room divisions; the overhanging, shade-giving roof, cantilevered outwards from its inset supports; as well as the *tokonoma* at the centre, where Wright located the fireplace – all aspects of the *interior* space of the 'Ho-o-den'. It is also interesting to note that this hybrid structure, joining as it does the temple and the house, may also have served as an inspiration for Wright's tendency 'to treat the dwelling as a form of temple to traditional family life – based around the "altar" or central communal hearth.'[9]

In addition to the direct effect of the 'Ho-o-den' on the 25-year-old Wright, the text for the Exposition catalogue on the 'Ho-o-den' was written by Okakura Kakuzo, later author of *The Book of Tea* (New York, 1906), a book that would have an enormous impact on Wright. The Exposition and its Japanese Pavilion also brought to Chicago America's leading authorities on Japanese art and architecture, including Silsbee's cousin Fenollosa and Edward Morse, author of the influential *Japanese Homes and their Surroundings* (London, 1885), with its numerous line drawings of traditional houses. Finally, the 'Ho-o-den' itself was neither dismantled nor burned in 1894, as were most of the structures of the Exposition, but remained on its lakefront island site until 1946, when Wright was almost 80.[10]

The same year as the opening of both the Exposition and his own office, Wright was invited to the house of his friend, and future repeat client, Edward Waller, banker for buildings such as Jenney's Home Insurance Company and Root's Monadnock and Rookery Buildings, who lived directly across the street from the Winslows in River Forest. There Wright was to meet 'Uncle Dan' Burnham (fresh from completing the Columbian Exposition and still searching for a designer to replace John Root), who had told Waller that Wright's Winslow House was a 'gentleman's house from grade to coping'. Related with overtones suggesting parallels to Christ's temptation by the devil, Wright almost 40 years later wrote how, after dinner, he was locked in the 'cozy' library with Waller and Burnham, who made him an unbelievable offer: Burnham, at that time perhaps the most powerful architect in America, would pay full expenses, and take care of Wright's family, while Wright studied for four years at the Ecole des Beaux-Arts in Paris, followed by two years living and studying in Rome, with the job of lead designer in Burnham's office upon his return.

Wright thought the offer was generous, splendid – and frightening, for what was being offered was also the promise of both guaranteed wealth and increased influence in a profession Burnham said would be changed by the success of the classical White City. After what must have been agonizing moments, Wright declined the offer, saying that Sullivan had spoiled him for the Beaux-Arts. To Burnham's objection that all of the great architects of the day favoured the classical, Wright recalls saying, 'if John Root were alive I don't believe he would feel that way about it. Richardson I am sure never would.' While we may doubt that Wright was quite so bold in naming Burnham's recently deceased partner, it is clear the offer was in fact made and declined, Wright's explanation coming with his parting words: 'I'm spoiled, first by birth, then by training, and [this had now come clear under pressure] by conviction, for anything like that.' Here Wright refers to the three great influences in his life up to that point: 'by birth' into the Lloyd Jones clan, 'by training' with Sullivan, and 'by conviction' learned from Emerson.[11]

At that moment in Chicago the choice to reject Burnham's offer must have seemed an astonishingly poor one, even to Wright. Before the Columbian Exposition opened, a deep economic depression, the worst up to that time in the country's history, had already begun. Three million souls were unemployed, 150 railways and 16,000 businesses, including the giant Illinois Steel Company, were closed. In Chicago itself, 20 per cent of the workers were laid off, 10 per cent of the inhabitants were threatened daily with starvation, and thousands of stores and offices stood empty. In what had been called the 'utopian' town of Pullman, rents and food costs kept rising even as wages were cut until, from May to July 1894, the nation's railways were shut down and the country paralysed by the Pullman strike, which was halted by the violent intervention of federal troops.

During this period the streets of Chicago were the training ground for an entirely new kind of newspaper writer: the investigative reporter. Chicago was the place that launched the careers of Stephen Crane, Theodore Dreiser, Lincoln Steffens, Ray Baker, George Ade, Jack London, Frank Norris, Jacob Riis, Robert Park and Peter Finley Dunne, who wrote a series of scathing satires of city life, dirty politics and social inequities that Dunne published under the pen-name 'Mr Dooley'. According to Dunne's Mr Dooley, a fictional Irish bartender who comments, in Irish brogue, on all matters large and small affecting Chicago's poor working-class citizens, the purpose of a newspaper 'should be to comfort the afflicted, and afflict the comfortable'.[12] John Lloyd Wright, Wright's second son, recalls that his father loved to read Mr Dooley aloud to the family, and that Wright 'would go into convulsions before he made much headway', laughing so hard he often could barely finish the story.[13]

William Stead, at that time 'the most celebrated reporter and moral reformer in the world', came to Chicago from London during his study tour of American newspapers, arriving the day after the Columbian Exposition closed. Appalled at the stark contrast between the White City and what he called 'the Black City' of Chicago's slums, Stead launched the first comprehensive investigation of the living conditions of the city's poor. After convening an extraordinary public meeting in November 1893, Stead established the Civic Federation 'to drive Satan from Chicago', its members including business leaders such as Marshall Field, the department store magnate, and Cyrus McCormick, Jr, the harvester manufacturer's heir, as well as social reformers such as Jane Addams and Jenkin Lloyd Jones. In February 1894 Stead published his book *If Christ Came to Chicago!*, a mix of radical religion and politics that served as a primary catalyst for the reform movement in Chicago.[14]

Due in no small part to the inequities documented by Stead and others, Chicago remained a thriving commercial centre. Each morning Wright's businessmen clients would return to their work in the city, and, in order to meet with them, Wright maintained an office in downtown Chicago for 25 years. In 1896, when Cecil Corwin left Chicago, Wright moved from the Schiller Building to Steinway Hall, where a group of younger architects, including Robert Spencer, Myron Hunt, George Dean, Richard Schmidt, Walter Burley Griffin, the brothers Allen and Irving Pond, and Dwight Perkins now had their offices. They and Wright were members of the Chicago Architectural Club, as well as part of a group that met at lunchtime in Perkins's office to discuss architecture and such related topics as Herbert Spencer's theories of social

Darwinism, Henry George's idea for a single tax, the political fortunes of the progressive party and politicians such as Robert La Follette of Wisconsin.[15] These young architects – Wright was 29 at the time he joined them – were all influenced by Sullivan, and were later given the name of the 'Prairie School'.

As we have seen, Wright shared with Sullivan a desire to develop an appropriate form of monumental architecture for the young democracy of America. Yet the primary legacy that Wright received from Sullivan and the Chicago School of architecture of which they were both a part was the steel-framed office building. As the product of private commercial interests and land speculation, the steel-framed skyscraper, while having a scale heretofore only given to public buildings, proved incapable of embodying either the monumental, or the space of appearance required for the existence of the public realm. Only when they took the form of multi-use or hybrid buildings, such as the Auditorium and the Schiller Building (the first true examples of this new building type),[16] which housed large, medium and small scale spaces – theatres, clubs and offices or hotel rooms – could the works of the Chicago School be considered monumental, embodying elements of the public realm.

While Wright had up to this point in his career focused primarily on house design – due to his 'moonlight' duties at Adler and Sullivan, his 'bootleg' commissions to pay the bills, and the steady stream of clients for houses now coming to his office – he was actually much closer to finding his own terms in the design of public buildings. This is indicated in Wright's remarkable design, only one year after opening his own practice, for the Monolithic Concrete Bank of 1894. The whole, though small, could not be more monumental, and was directly related to the forms of Egyptian temples. As its name makes clear, this small but powerful cubic space was to be built of concrete, which, rather than being clad, was to be left exposed – a radical idea at the time. The singularity of the interior space, and the manner in which it is born of a fusion of its form, structure and material, is exactly the opposite of the steel-frame office building.

The relative freedom Wright felt in designing public buildings, where the similarities among people are recognized, as opposed to houses, where the differences between people are highlighted, is evident in his unrealized design for the Wolf Lake Amusement Park, commissioned by Edward Waller in 1895. This series of pavilions arrayed around a semicircular canal and on a circular island at the centre can be understood as a systematic composition of unique places, variations on the theme of the cruciform interlocking of spaces. Close examination of the pavilions reveals plan fragments similar to a number of Wright's later Prairie Period designs, including Unity Temple, the Darwin Martin House and even the Imperial Hotel.

Wright's evolution of the new American monument took a huge leap forward when, in 1897, Wright was commissioned by his uncle Jenkin Lloyd Jones to build a new All Souls Church, now to be redefined as an urban social services centre, with the sanctuary as its main gathering space. This change in the mission of Jones's institution was reflected in the change of its name, which took place during Wright's design process, to the Abraham Lincoln Center. The original All Souls Church, built by Silsbee only ten years before, had evolved into a neighbourhood social centre, where religious and reform leaders were already gathering when Wright first came to Chicago. What Jones envisioned now was an 'institutional church', with the sanctuary as an auditorium housed in a seven-storey hybrid building, along with meeting rooms, classrooms and social services offices. The office building was understood by Jones to have more modern and secular associations, and to be more engaged in daily urban life, than the historicist architecture of the typical church building.[17]

Wright's final design of 1899 for the Abraham Lincoln Center is both an astonishing breakthrough and an exceptionally comprehensive resolution of the hybrid building type. The overall structure of seven floors employs Sullivan's skyscraper expression of vertical brick piers with recessed windows and walls between, yet both the sanctuary, on the first and second floors, and the large entry hall at the ground floor, are also framed by piers set in from the outer edge of the building. The result is that the front elevation reveals a series of volumes inside volumes, allowing all the various spaces to read clearly, irrespective of their widely varying size – something Sullivan and the Chicago School had been unable to accomplish. In addition, the offices at the top of the building had stairs in each of the building's four corners and were linked by a skylighted open space at their centre (exactly as in Wright's later Larkin Building), while the sanctuary was framed by four free-standing piers, with light introduced from high clerestory windows and entry at the edge and not the centre, to either side of the pulpit (exactly as in Wright's later Unity Temple).

Despite his uncle's statement that Wright had masterfully solved the problem set him, Jones continued to make what can only be seen in retrospect as entirely unreasonable demands on his nephew to change the design. In order to preserve his relationship with his favourite uncle, Wright eventually withdrew from the Abraham Lincoln Center commission, allowing Dwight Perkins to be credited with the final building, a stripped-down version of his design. That Jenkin Lloyd Jones later felt considerable remorse at this episode is indicated by the powerful support he would give Wright's design for Unity Temple, both in endorsing Wright's receipt of the commission and in defending his innovative design and its unusual method of construction.

In 1895 Wright had received the commission to design a series of patterned forms into which were cast specially formed glass blocks, which acted to bounce light inwards, for the Luxfer Prism Company, as well as designing a prototypical skyscraper utilizing the Luxfer Prisms. As has been recently shown, the glass block

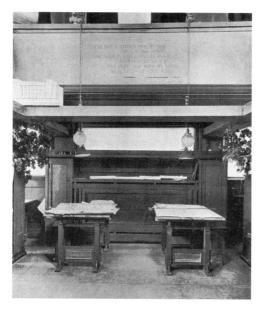

Photo of interior of the Frank Lloyd Wright Studio, Oak Park, *c.* 1908; model of Larkin Building at upper left.

patterns Wright developed, which are documented in the files of the US Patent Office, indicate his knowledge and understanding of the most ancient ordering geometries, developed from his Froebel training, his studies of *The Grammar of Ornament*, and in particular his work with Sullivan – geometries that he would employ for the rest of his career.[18]

The substantial fee from the Luxfer Prisms commission also allowed Wright to begin work on the addition of a studio, library and office to his Oak Park house. Completed in 1897, the studio complex, entered through a low loggia off Chicago Avenue, consisted of a double-height, top-lit, drafting room to the left, square in plan at the base with an octagon-shaped mezzanine above; a library to the right, octagonal in plan and lit by high clerestory windows; and Wright's private office directly ahead. The Studio, as it was called, was connected to the Wright house by a hallway in which an existing willow tree was allowed to pierce the roof, a kind of magical passageway through which Wright's children would appear in the Studio at the most inopportune moments, to the chagrin of their father and the amusement of the draughtsmen.

In the announcement of the official opening of his office in Root's Rookery Building, where he moved from the Steinway Building in 1898, the tremendous energy and time Wright was putting into his practice becomes apparent in his posted office hours: Monday through Saturday, at the Oak Park Studio 8.00 to 11.00 am; a train ride downtown, Rookery Building 12.00 noon to 2.00 pm; back to Oak Park, where he had office hours every evening from 5.00 pm to 9.00 pm. Wright's employees worked at the Oak Park Studio, where all design and documentation was done, while he used the Rookery Building office for client meetings, it being convenient to their downtown offices. Wright's suburban house clients could also meet him in Oak Park after work. In addition, the announcement states that 'clients and those with a kindred interest in architecture will also be welcome in the suburban studio during business hours, where provision has been made for their reception and entertainment.'[19]

Finally, we should not forget the hours of design work (the rule rather than the exception) that Wright recalled undertaking alone at night in the Studio, in order that the draughtsmen would have things to work on the next morning. Wright's son Lloyd later recalled,

I can remember night after night . . . he'd come up [to his room] dead tired, dead tired because he was struggling on the [drawing] board himself – nobody else – at night because there was no interference . . . and he would come up and go to bed at two or three o'clock in the morning night after night, day after day, week after week, month after month, year after year.[20]

Lloyd also remembered that Wright kept a piano in the studio, so that, both day and night, music could be his source of refreshment from his labours at the drawing board. This demanding schedule, exceptional both at the time and today, would be typical for Wright most of his life, and his best time for designing would remain the dark hours of night, after everyone else had gone to bed.

In this early period of his practice Wright found much of his work in the suburbs to which the families of the wealthier citizens of Chicago were fleeing, especially in Saints' Rest, as his own home of Oak Park was known. Despite the economic depression, people were still building houses and apartments. During the first six years after he set up his own practice in 1893, Wright built twelve single family houses and six apartment buildings, as well as one public project. He also designed 23 unbuilt projects, establishing a pattern of unbuilt works equalling or outpacing built works that would remain fairly constant throughout his 65-year career. While the Francis Apartments, built in Chicago in 1895, are fairly typical of the period, the Francisco Terrace Apartments, built for Edward Waller in Chicago in 1895, gathered the apartments around a spacious interior court with corner stairs and entry to the first-floor units via an open-air balcony walkway – perhaps the earliest example of what would later be called a 'street in the air', a concept considered highly innovative when it was deployed in European projects 25 years later.

In searching for a new and more appropriate model for both the multi-family apartment building and the single family house, Wright was hardly alone. Since 1873 Chicago had been the centre of a growing awareness of the importance of the home in the structure of society. Yet in 1893, the year Wright opened his own practice, there was a sea change in this movement, stimulated by the appalling conditions in Chicago's slums, the total lack of planning in the new suburbs, the arrival of new building and hygiene technology, and the emergence of new conceptions of the family – in particular of the role of the housewife.[21]

Wright's first public lectures, given in 1894 and 1896, engage what was then the very latest thinking on the house, including the concepts of integrating with the natural site; simpler roof-forms;

introduction of sunlight to the interior; being smaller and simpler in organization; containing as few rooms as possible – eliminating the parlour and collecting all family activities, including dining and entertainment of guests, into one large living room; using built-in and machine-made furniture; integrating services within the fabric of the house, such as building in heating radiators under windows; employment of newly available, 'truly modern' and 'matchless' plumbing fixtures; and efficient, well-organized kitchens – which Wright already calls the 'working department' and 'laboratory'. In this Wright employed the nomenclature of the housing reformers, as well as his own ideal of an indigenous architecture that achieves both utility and beauty.[22]

Among the residences of this period, most notable are the Isidore Heller House of 1896 in Chicago, where the living and dining rooms are each cruciform in plan, linked by the entry hall, and the Joseph Husser House of 1899, a elegantly resolved composition of geometrically independent rooms aligned along a central axis. In the Husser design, Wright employed as his 'model' for reinterpretation Richardson's Winn Memorial Library of 1877 in Woburn, Massachusetts, a building he may have seen under construction when he was living in nearby Weymouth. Between these two well-resolved houses, however, Wright made a series of designs, including those for Peter Goan, Jesse Baldwin, Nathan Moore, Chauncey Williams, George Furbeck and Rollin Furbeck, that appear ever more uncertain and even chaotic in their formal composition.

The cause for this slow but certain unravelling of Wright's design process during this period was his belief, stated in his 1894 lecture, that 'there should be as many types of homes as there are types of people, for it is the individuality of the occupants that should give character and color to the building;'[23] that he should provide a unique and different design for each of his clients. Wright's conception of the design of the family house, recently characterized as 'the architecture of portraiture'[24] – using Wright's own parallel between his designing a house for and John Singer Sargent's painting a portrait of their respective clients – proved impossible for Wright to sustain, at least in his original way of defining it, in the face of his ever-increasing number of commissions.

By 1899 the strain of his burgeoning practice and his growing family, now with five children (son David came in 1895 and daughter Frances in 1898) had begun to weigh on Wright. In order to allow his practice to thrive, his wife and he had strictly separated their respective spheres of influence, so that, despite operating on the same Oak Park site, 'a division' began to grow between them. Exacerbating the situation for Catherine was Wright's tendency to purchase luxuries before necessities, which, given the family's escalating expenses, had led to the embarrassment of unpaid grocery bills amounting to thousands of dollars. In addition, Wright used his own house and studio as his primary place for experimentation: there was no end to his tearing out and rebuilding in every room. Anyone who has lived for even a short while with the dust, noise and inconvenience of renovation can only imagine how difficult these years in Oak Park must have been for Catherine.

Wright felt more and more remote from his wife and family, even admitting that one night at dinner when Warren McArthur, early client and friend, caught one of the children and called out, 'Quick now, Frank, what's the name of this one?' he had given the wrong name. Writing more than 30 years later, Wright claims that, as to being a father, 'I am afraid I never looked the part. Nor ever acted it. I didn't feel it. And I didn't know how.'[25] But these feelings were not yet evident to any except Wright himself.

More representative during this time are the memories of Wright's son John, who wrote of his father: 'He was an epic of wit and merriment that gave our home the feeling of a jolly carnival. He had a way of his own of wringing a laugh from tears, and turning frowns into smiles.' John remembers the Wright house being filled with music, laughter and 'a round of parties', this despite

Wright's long and exhausting hours of office work. In fact Wright seemed to have no end of time and patience for his large brood of often poorly behaved offspring, and John wrote that Wright 'was preeminently a lover of home and family', who 'lived the perfect family life'.[26]

Wright had in 1894 built the Playroom onto the first floor of his house, so that his children would have a space of their own, and so his wife could give Froebel training to the neighbourhood children. The Playroom was a beautiful space with a barrel-vaulted ceiling above, brick interior walls, low-set bands of windows with built-in seats along two sides of the vault, a piano built into the wall at one end, and on the other end wall a mural of the *Fisherman and the Genie*, based upon Wright's geometric interpretation of the *Arabian Nights*.

During the period when Wright was struggling to achieve clarity of function and simplicity of composition in his architectural designs for houses, he was every afternoon instructing his own children in the Froebel system, reading again the instructional manuals provided for the teacher. At some point this became more than a diversion for Wright, for here in the Froebel training was a way of making that did not rely on the seemingly endless series of unique formal inventions his belief in the necessity for 'a different design for each different client' seemed to require. On the contrary, the Froebel training proposed that making should engage only a limited number of elements and spatial types, which were employed as the themes for variation, as in music. In this way Wright's later re-immersion in the Froebel training may be seen as instrumental in his breakthrough to what would be recognized as his greatest innovation of this period – the Prairie House.

4

Prairie House and the Progressive Movement 1899–1909

Wright's breakthrough, at the age of 32, to what he named 'the Prairie House' occurred exactly with the opening of the new millennium, and was part of the radical changes then sweeping the entire world. In two prototypical houses commissioned in 1900 by the Curtis Publishing Company for publication in *The Ladies' Home Journal*, and in the versions of each designed and built that same year for the Warren Hickox and Harley Bradley families in Kankakee, Illinois, Wright arrived at the two cruciform plan 'types' that would serve as the starting point for nearly all the Prairie Houses that followed. It has been convincingly shown that both these plans were developed directly from the simple little 'four-square' plan of Wright's own house of 1889.[1] With this an important change in his design process had occurred, for Wright had moved from using the works of other architects as 'models' or starting points to employing his own designs as the themes for variation.

Wright's Prairie Houses were characterized by exceptional spatial freedom, rigorous formal order, and a combination of usefulness and comfort heretofore unknown in either the Old or New World. The Prairie Houses were soon recognized as both setting a new standard for the American house, elegantly solving all the challenges posed by the 'model' or reformed home movement, as well as being the first examples of a truly modern architecture for the new millennium, 'a definite answer ... to those questions which many of the most advanced buildings of the day seemed to exist merely to propose.'[2]

Yet Wright's publication of these two seminal designs in *The Ladies' Home Journal*, a popular women's magazine with a national readership of one million (the largest circulation in the country at the time) and great influence among homemakers, rather than in a professional architectural journal, was nothing if not carefully calculated. Indeed, for the rest of his career Wright would consistently present his designs for domestic living to the widest possible audiences – directing his accompanying texts to those considering building their own homes, and to home-building companies, rather than to the architects who might be employed to design them. Through *The Ladies' Home Journal, House Beautiful, House and Garden, House and Home, Life* and other homemaker magazines, with whose editors, such as Edward Bok of *The Ladies' Home Journal*, he developed long and close relationships, Wright presented his ideas directly to potential clients, while also avoiding being represented as part of a larger and more anonymous architectural profession.

The first of *The Ladies' Home Journal* houses, which Wright called 'A Home in a Prairie Town', was published in February 1901. The plan, as Wright wrote, 'was arranged to offer the least resistance to a simple mode of living, in keeping with a high ideal of the family life together.' The low, horizontally extended exterior, with its deep sheltering roof overhangs all around, 'recognizes the influence of the prairie, is firmly and broadly associated with the site, and makes a feature of [the landscape's] quiet level.'[3] Wright's vision for this new American house was comprehensive, as is indicated by the fact that he opens his text with a proposal for an ideal 'prairie community', and closes it with a description of all major materials of construction – and a modest price of $6,970.

The second of *The Ladies' Home Journal* houses, published in July 1901, was rather sarcastically named 'A Small House with "Lots of Room in It"', a reference to the unreasonable (though common) client demand for houses to be smaller and less expensive, yet at the same time providing both more space and unique 'features'.

Priced at a very modest $5,835, this house was well within the reach of the middle class, and the accompanying site plans showed the house in alternate positions on a standard 100-foot (30 m) lot, rather than as a part of an ideal community.[4]

The plans of both prototypical houses were cruciform in shape, evolved from Wright's own Oak Park house, and unfold their projecting and pinwheeling spaces from a massive central fireplace, so that one moves from room to room along the edges, at the corners. The cruciform plans open out in four directions 'to take advantage of light, air, and prospect, the enjoyable things one goes to the suburbs to secure', providing light and views on three sides of the primary family rooms – to this day an exceptional condition in house design, but one that would be the norm for Wright.

This connection to nature, the positive reason families were moving to the suburbs, remained for Wright the primary inspiration for his Prairie Houses. Yet in the suburbs where his houses were being built, the pre-existing natural landscape had been subdivided into lots by streets and utilities, and all too often most of the indigenous trees and vegetation had been removed. These suburbs were far indeed from being 'natural' places, and Wright conceived of the architect's task in designing houses for the American suburbs to be one of reconstitution of a lost natural balance, a nature now fundamentally and permanently changed through the inhabitation of man.

In a lecture titled 'Concerning Landscape Architecture', given in 1900 to a women's civic organization in Oak Park (where, Wright noted, nature was expected 'to behave herself and not set a bad example to the children'), Wright argued for honouring the inherent nature of each type of indigenous plant and tree, as in the work of Gertrude Jekyll, the English landscape designer whose *Home and Garden*, published that same year, he cited. Wright argued that landscape and architecture were equally important in creating a community, and that the natural environment was more influential

on our character than 'the cultivated conduct of good society –
though indeed the two are not that widely separated. You will find
the environment reflecting unerringly the society.'5

Wright's site plans for his houses from this period, with their
careful preservation of existing trees, precisely sculpted lawns,
terraces and walled gardens overflowing with 'informal masses of
foliage and bloom', have until recently been largely ignored. Thus
we are surprised to find that Wright's Prairie Houses were often
located at the edge of their suburban sites, so as to allow their
gardens to occupy the geometric centre of the sites – a privileged
position normally reserved for the house itself. In this way Wright
was able to weave together exterior and interior spaces through the
carefully choreographed entry sequence, as well as through the
daily rituals of family life, so that the house and landscape were inextricably bound to one another. Rather than making free-standing
objects in the landscape, as is so distressingly typical today, Wright
constructed a remarkable interdependence between house and
landscape, such that neither appears complete without the other.

During this decade Wright designed 130 Prairie Houses, of
which exactly half were realized; the vast majority of those 65 were
built in the rapidly growing American suburbs. While Wright is
often credited with the invention of the particular American architectural type, the single-family house, he is rarely credited with
conceiving the first comprehensive designs for the American suburb where these houses were destined to be built. In fact Wright
'begins at the beginning' of his 1900 'A Home in a Prairie Town'
text by presenting his design for a suburban community, a series of
400-foot (120 m) square blocks each of which has four of Wright's
prototypical houses arranged in a pinwheel formation on four
200-foot (60 m) square sites – a little less than an acre each. In
this 'quadruple block plan', each house faced a different direction,
allowing both a broad 'prospect to the community as a whole and
absolute privacy'.

Portrait of Wright, *c.* 1908, aged 49.

Wright believed the community must be designed with the house, leading to this design for an integrated suburban community, where houses were clustered together to provide large open natural spaces, and where circulation of horse-drawn vehicles (later cars) and pedestrians were separated. The degree to which, in these plans, made well before the 1908 arrival of Henry Ford's Model T, the first mass-production automobile, Wright anticipated the automobile's emergence as the primary agent of change in the American landscape is nothing short of astonishing. Wright's larger intentions become clear when we realize that his 1900 'prairie community' plan was grounded in the mile-square 'Jeffersonian' grid that was employed to order the entirety of America west of the Missouri and Mississippi rivers following the Louisiana Purchase of 1803.

The Studio in Oak Park, in which the designs of the Prairie Houses were conceived during this decade, was made up of a small group of talented young draughtsmen and women including Marion Mahony, the first practising woman architect in Illinois, William Drummond, Francis 'Barry' Byrne, George Willis, Walter Burley Griffin, Andrew Willatzen, Harry Robinson, John Van Bergen, Charles White, Albert McArthur, along with office manager Isabel Roberts. During this period Wright's Studio of around ten members produced designs for an average of twenty-one projects each year, of which an average of eleven were built, meaning that a set of drawings was completed every two-and-a-half weeks, and a building was constructed every four-and-a-half weeks.

Several of Wright's draughtsmen had been educated in what was called 'pure design' by Emil Lorch at the Chicago School of Architecture, housed in the Art Institute. 'Pure design', developed in Chicago, was an art educational programme based upon the pedagogic techniques of Alden Wesley Dow, among others, who analysed Oriental ornamental patterns in search of first principles. Closely paralleling Froebel kindergarten training, this method of instruction was highly abstract: 'Lorch's innovation was that he sought architectural bedrock in patterns and conventionalizations of nature rather than in function or statics.'[6]

In these early years the Studio was organized much like an atelier, where Wright initiated each design, which was then developed, under his watchful eye, by an individual draughtsman. All the work of the studio was discussed and critiqued by the group, and Wright respected the talents of those working with him. While Wright was clearly by far the best designer in the Studio, and the principal of the practice, his designs were nevertheless not above constructive criticism from his junior colleagues. This reflects the fact that Wright's initial experiences in private practice took place in collective atelier-like environments, with colleagues whom he considered his equals.

With office hours every evening until 9.00 pm, Wright intended the Studio in Oak Park, like the Steinway Hall atelier, to also be a place where architects, clients and friends could meet and discuss architecture as well as the larger issues of the day. The Studio, Office and, particularly, the little Library were walk-in exemplifications of Wright's system of design, carefully ordered and arrayed with Japanese woodblock prints, ceramics, as well as models, drawings, and leaded glass windows of his own designs. Wright used these spaces and their contents to educate his clients, his draughtsmen and himself: for he believed architecture was a discipline whose perfection required extensive daily practice, as one must practice a piano.

Wright practised on whatever material lay closest at hand. He would stop work each day and lead the draughtsmen out into the surrounding woods and fields to collect wild flowers and prairie grasses, which he would then arrange according to his studies of the ancient Japanese art of *Ikebana*, the results displayed in the studio. His son John tells of Wright bringing home dozens of gas-filled balloons and spending hours in the vaulted Playroom arranging the brightly coloured spheres in different patterns by tying them to furniture and playing out their strings to varying lengths.[7] He insisted on arranging different and ever more dynamic compositions using the dining table, chairs, tablecloth, napkins, glasses and silver – all of which he had designed, as a result delaying many a meal in the Wright household. Wright's clients often tell how, during his periodic visits to their houses, he would completely rearrange their furniture into a dynamic new order – a gift from their architect.

In addition to the non-stop renovations on his house and Studio during these years, Wright regularly rearranged the furniture in his own home, his designs taking the form of dynamic compositions playing off against the regular geometries of the rooms, with the furniture set in asymmetrical, pinwheeling yet balanced formations,

An exhibition of Frank Lloyd Wright work at the Art Institute, *c.* 1907, including a display of leaded glass for the Martin House, Buffalo, New York.

and rugs starting in one room and ending in another, all as if to suggest the positions and movements of the occupants themselves. While this may appear to have been mere play, it was in fact for Wright very serious play, a series of experiments exploring ever more dynamic interactions of space and occupation – the experience of architecture. After completing each arrangement, Wright, an avid photographer who owned a number of cameras and employed photographic analogies in his lectures starting in 1896, would document his furniture composition with a photograph, and then rearrange it all over again.

Wright was a member of the Architectural Club of Chicago, which had begun as an informal sketching club in 1885 and had been officially named in 1895. Starting in 1887, the year Wright arrived in Chicago, they organized exhibitions in rooms at the Art Institute, showing work by their members as well as examples from around the world, including fourteen works by British Arts and Crafts architect Charles Robert Ashbee in 1900. During this period Wright's work would dominate these exhibitions, particularly in 1907, when it was almost a one-man show, to a degree that often brought criticism to the Club. The Architectural Club, unlike the American Institute of Architects and the various builders' clubs, was focused not on business but on design – the solution of social problems through architecture. In 1899 the Architectural Club merged with other similar clubs to form the Architectural League of America, with the motto 'Progress before Precedent'. Wright gave two lectures at this new group's annual meeting in Chicago in 1900, and in the second he argued that the architect who designs a small house that combines use, comfort and utility 'has more valuable [work] experience than he who builds a city with the pomp and circumstance of established forms' – a clear shot at Burnham.[8]

It was during this period that Wright's work began to receive both national and international attention. In 1900 Wright's friend and fellow architect from Steinway Hall, Robert Spenser, had published the first extensive presentation of Wright's work in the *Architectural Review*, a Boston journal. That same year, Ashbee, who was touring America for the British National Trust, met Wright at a Hull House dinner sponsored by the Arts and Crafts Society. Ashbee, his wife and mother visited with the Wrights in Oak Park, and in their journal they remembered the Wrights as being a splendid family. Wright was the only architect Ashbee mentioned in his official report on the trip, and the friendship they then formed endured for decades. In turn, and despite his later disclaimers, Wright had already long been influenced by architectural ideas coming from Europe, especially those in the British journal *The Studio*, which began publication in 1893, and focused on the Arts and Crafts works, inspired by John Ruskin and William Morris, of such British architects as C.F.A. Voysey, Baillie Scott, Charles Rennie Mackintosh, Sir Edwin Lutyens and Ashbee.

It was to a meeting of the Arts and Crafts Society at Hull House that Wright gave what many still consider one of his most important lectures, titled 'The Art and Craft of the Machine', in March 1901. Wright opened by paying homage to Ruskin and Morris, whom he calls 'the two great reformers of modern times'. Yet his lecture both embraced and attacked the British Arts and Craft Movement, the chief exponent of which, Morris, had ruled out the use of machines in the making of architectural crafts and ornament. Wright argued for the absolutely necessary place of the machine in modern art and architecture, and talked movingly about Chicago, where the iron furnaces glow late into the night and the swing-bridge (a memory from his first night) makes its 'stately passage' across the river. Wright argued that the straight-line rectangular cuts of sawmill machines will provide the wood trim of the modern age, free of any decorative pattern save the natural grain of the wood itself. As he had in his first five public lectures, Wright repeatedly defined architecture as a kind of weaving, reconceived in modern terms.[9]

This early lecture also indicates the manner in which, in his work and thought, Wright was simultaneously engaging both the machine and nature as paradigms for architectural design. Yet the tension between the technological and the natural, identified in the writings of Thoreau, would later be recognized as the fundamental conflict within American culture.[10] Wright's resolution of this dichotomy was possible because his 'vision of nature emphasizes its abstract and even mathematical qualities, while his vision of the machine is highly organic.'[11]

Hidden in this lecture, and rarely noticed, is a revelation of Wright's self-image at the time, one connected to his use of Victor Hugo's *Notre Dame de Paris* of 1832. Having read the book as a child,

Wright was surprised to discover in 1888, in the edition in the All Souls library, the chapter titled 'Ceci Tuera Cela', or 'this will kill that'. Here Hugo, in a passage that profoundly affected Wright, speaks directly to the reader of the Gothic cathedral's capacity to embody the monumental, to be the 'great book of stone' for humankind.[12] Hugo states that, up until the fifteenth century, 'the material and intellectual forces of society all converged on that one point: architecture', and that 'whoever was then born to be a poet, became an architect', because 'architecture was the principal register of mankind, that during that period all ideas of any complexity which arose in the world became a building.'

Hugo tells how, in the fifteenth century, everything changed with the invention of the printing press, and 'the human mind discovered a means of perpetuating itself which was not only more lasting and resistant than architecture, but also simpler and easier . . . The book was to kill the building.' Yet this new means of perpetuating ideas did not possess the place-making qualities of the monument after which Hugo's story is named: 'In the days of architecture, thought had turned into a mountain and taken powerful hold of a century and of a place. Now it turned into a flock of birds and was scattered on the four winds.' Hugo describes what happened to architecture after this event, how:

> from the sixteenth century on, architecture's malady became apparent; it was no longer the essential expression of society; it turned miserably into a classical art . . . once it was true and modern, now it became pseudo-antique. This is the decadence we call the Renaissance . . . it is the setting sun which we all take to be the dawn.

Here Hugo suggests that all is lost, that 'architecture is dead, dead beyond recall, killed by the printed book', yet in the very next paragraph he holds out hope, making a strange prophesy: 'The great accident of an architect of genius might occur in the twentieth century just like that of Dante in the thirteenth.' Up to this point in the text Wright, in his Hull House lecture, had fairly accurately paraphrased Hugo. Now Wright made a revealing modification to Hugo's timetable: 'if architecture arise again, reconstruct, as Hugo prophesies she may do *in the latter days of the nineteenth century*'.[13] Wright's combination of the missionary and the messianic, aggravated by the fact that, as a Lloyd Jones, he could be nothing other than a revolutionary architect, can be seen in his reaction to Hugo's story of the death and possible rebirth of his beloved mother-art, architecture. Now aged 34, did Wright, as is suggested by his change in Hugo's prophesized date to make it better fit his own biography, see himself as the 'architect of genius' who could revive architecture?

Hull House, America's second settlement house, had been opened in 1889 by Jane Addams, and by 1900 it had become not only a centre for social work in the poor neighbourhoods that surrounded it, but also a cultural meeting place for the progressive citizens of the city. In preparing to open Hull House, Addams had visited Tolstoy on his farm in rural Russia as well as London's Toynbee Hall, where Ashbee developed his own social ideas about art. Hull House was the venue for a remarkably large number of social and cultural clubs and lectures, including art, traditional handicrafts, music, various political and philosophical clubs, and the Arts and Crafts Society, of which Wright was a charter member when it opened in 1894. In addition to conducting research into the living conditions of the city's poor, working to rewrite laws and regulations so as to improve health and sanitation, and campaigning against dirty politicians, the residents of Hull House hosted numerous lectures by both visiting experts and local leaders, including many of the faculty at the recently opened University of Chicago.[14]

In many ways the social and political activities at Addams's Hull House paralleled those that, since 1886, had taken place at Wright's uncle Jenkin Lloyd Jones's All Souls Church (renamed the Abraham Lincoln Center in 1905), and both were centres of the progressive movement in Chicago. Among those who visited both institutions were Susan B. Anthony, Booker T. Washington, William Jennings Bryan and Robert La Follette, and together the two centres addressed issues ranging from prohibition to racial injustice, education, women's suffrage, housing improvement, poverty relief, political reform and pacifism.

Another lecturer at Hull House was John Dewey, a contemporary of Wright and a faculty member at the University of Chicago, who would later be recognized as the greatest American philosopher. Upon his arrival in Chicago in 1894 Dewey had written, 'Chicago is the place to make you appreciate at every turn the absolute opportunity which chaos affords – it is sheer Matter with no standards at all', and yet Dewey's pragmatic philosophy would be deeply affected by 'the general utilitarian idealism of Chicago'. Wright maintained an office in downtown Chicago through the entire period Dewey lived and worked there, and he and Dewey crossed paths repeatedly. Initiated during his eleven years in Chicago, and inspired by William James, Emerson and Whitman, Dewey's philosophy of living consisted of three primary concepts, each of which had enormous influence on Wright.

The first was Dewey's lifelong dedication to reforming education, which emphasized learning through doing and making, modelled on craft apprenticeship and acting to join, rather than separate, mind and body. In this Dewey was inspired by Colonel Francis Parker's famous experimental school in Chicago, started in 1883. The second was Dewey's redefinition of what it meant to be an American citizen, holding that it was every individual's responsibility to bring democracy into being through their everyday actions and experience; his argument for the equal importance of the individual and their community; and his evolution of a conception of 'organic democracy', a uniquely American form of democracy then striving to 'achieve itself on a vaster scale, and in a more thorough and final way, than history has previously witnessed.'

Finally, and of the greatest significance to Wright, was Dewey's emphasis of the integrative *experience* as the only appropriate mode of evaluating the world and everything present in it; his belief that all art had an ethical imperative to 'construct the good'; and his investigations of non-Western cultures (it is intriguing to note that Dewey and Wright would both live in the Orient from 1919 to 1921).[15] The influence of Dewey's liberal progressive philosophy can be found in Wright's work throughout his life, and it appears inspiration flowed both ways; in Dewey's classic *Art as Experience* (1934), the architectural examples bear a resemblance, far too close to be coincidental, to Wright's buildings.

The writings of two other liberal progressive thinkers on the University of Chicago faculty would have an effect on Wright, and reflected the issues facing Chicago in this period. Thorstein Veblen's *The Theory of the Leisure Class* (1899), a savage satire of the upper middle class in Chicago, demonstrated that what he termed conspicuous consumption and predatory economic exploit motivated all aspects of life, and particularly the mode of dress and the design of houses.[16] Robert Ezra Park, who started as a newspaper reporter and helped found the nation's first department of sociology in Chicago, established the concept of 'urban ecology' and proposed that the city was simultaneously 'a product of nature', 'a kind of social organism' and 'the workshop of civilization'. While agreeing with Dewey that face-to-face association with one's immediate neighbours was the definition of a community, Park also acknowledged that 'commerce and communication, banks and newspapers' now acted to bind the larger world together, and warned as early as 1916 that 'the most demoralizing single instrument of present-day civilization is the automobile'.[17]

During this period Wright usually attracted clients who decidedly did not fit into Veblen's 'leisure class', which was composed of those who studiously conformed to the prevailing taste in all matters. Rather, Wright's clients were most often independent-minded social and business mavericks with whom Wright seemed to have an immediate connection. Wright's designs for the Prairie Houses and their furnishings are powerful crystallizations of the rituals of daily family life, as exemplified by his dining tables, with their corner light posts and high-backed chairs literally creating a room within a room, a protected, perfected place for the family to gather at the end of the workday. While later often characterized as dictatorial in his dealings with his clients, their testimony is exactly the opposite. On this Wright was clear: 'Human use and comfort should not be taxed to pay dividends to any "designer's" idiosyncrasy. Human use and comfort should have intimate possession of every interior.'[18]

In 1902, probably inspired by Wright's 65 works she saw displayed in the Art Institute Exhibit, Susan Lawrence Dana, a 48-year-old widow who had recently inherited her family's fortune, hired Wright to build her home in Springfield, Illinois. The rooms of the Dana House are remarkably open, one to another, and movement takes place through them, rather than via connecting corridors, encouraging chance meetings and a shared experience of the spaces of the house. During the preceding two centuries architecture had been relying more and more on corridors and one-door rooms, increasingly emphasizing functional separation and individual privacy. Yet in the Dana House, as in the Prairie Houses in general, Wright opposed this by constructing 'an architecture arising out of the deep fascination that draws people towards others; and architecture that recognizes passion, carnality, and sociality.'[19] The result is what might best be described as a familial relation among the various rooms of the house, an example of Wright's idealized vision of family life taking place.

The Martin House site plan, 1903, Buffalo, New York, as redrawn for the 1910 Wasmuth publication.

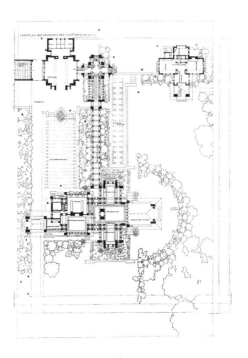

After Wright had designed a house in Oak Park for his brother William, Darwin Martin hired Wright to design for Buffalo, New York, both his family house and the headquarters of the Larkin Company, of which he was chief executive officer. The Martin House of 1903, designed when Wright was 36 years old, is an extraordinary achievement and marks a high point in his Prairie period. The complex of five separate structures, including a house for Martin's sister, all linked by a pergola and interlocked with gardens, is ordered by an exquisitely crafted site plan with a series of cruciform pavilions, the axes of which are woven together to produce a matrix of places in the landscape. Wright felt this site plan was as near perfection as he was able to achieve, and he kept this drawing on the wall of his drafting room for the next fifty years.

The Robie House,
Chicago, Illinois,
1908, exterior view
from southeast.

The Robie House,
dining-room period
photograph; all
furniture designed
by Wright.

The interior spaces of the Martin House are not so much contained as woven, and inhabitants seem to have entered a forest of pier-trunks and free-spanning beam-limbs, the daylight flickering through the lines of leaded glass windows and reflected from the gold-leaf pressed into the horizontal joints of the brick. Those inside, protected within the shadows made by the overhanging sheltering roofs, can at the same time see outside in all directions through the continuous bands of windows, providing a simultaneous sense of refuge and prospect – the precise characteristics later found to be required to provide comfort and repose for those inhabiting the prairie landscape.[20]

Frederick Robie, inventor and president of the Excelsior Manufacturing Company, which made bicycles, was ten years younger than Wright when he hired him to build his Chicago house in 1908. Wright and Robie shared a passion for machines and speed, both owning early versions of steam-powered automobiles, and Robie later said, 'from the first we had a definite community of thought. When I talked in mechanical terms he talked and thought in architectural terms. I thought, well, he was in my world.'[21] The house, which Robie called 'one of the cleanest business deals I ever had', is most famous for its single large space, with living room and dining room separated only by a free-standing fireplace and full-height glass doors running the full length of the room along the south side, and for its exceptionally daring cantilevered roof overhangs to the east and west, structured by hidden steel beams.

That such an extraordinarily beautiful design, built in 1909, would also be tailored so precisely to the environment that on 21 June, the longest day of the year, the sun is shaded by the roof so as to just touch the bottom edge of the south-facing glass doors, and on 21 December, the shortest day of the year, the sun penetrates all the way across the living and dining room, warming the concrete floor, came as a shock in 1969 to those who assumed energy efficiency had only recently been discovered as a determinant of architectural form.[22] But for Wright, trained in the tradition of practice, poetic and practical intentions, today invariably assumed to be mutually exclusive, are always to be accomplished simultaneously, so as to render the more practical intention (shading of glass) unremarkable, while rendering the more poetic aspect (plastic expression of cantilever in space) remarkable.

The Avery Coonleys of Riverside, the Chicago suburb designed by Olmstead, chose Wright as their architect in 1907 because Queene Ferry Coonley said she perceived in his work 'the countenance of principle'. In the Coonley House, which Wright described as his best design, he raised the entire living floor to the second level, where an extraordinary series of pavilion-like rooms, sheltered under the gently folded roof planes, was ordered so as to allow Mrs Coonley to meet her Christian Scientist patients in private. Mrs Coonley was also very interested in progressive education, and Wright designed a playhouse and kindergarten for what he and the Coonleys conceived would be a new type of ex-urban social and cultural centre for the American suburb. Wright collaborated on this project with the Chicago landscape architect Jens Jensen, who was at that time developing a parallel indigenous American school of landscape design, focusing on the use of native plants and integration with the natural topography.

Although attention is most often focused on these larger houses, it should be remembered that the vast majority of the Prairie Houses were built for middle-class clients with modest budgets. It is also important to note that Wright considered the limitations of the budgets and programmes of these modest houses to be 'the architect's best friends', a belief he first stated in 1900. Among the dozens of modest Prairie Houses, all of which incorporated the thinking of progressive reformers of the time, we should cite in particular the L. K. Horner House, the Mrs Thomas Gale House, the Isabel Roberts House, the Robert Evans House, the Thomas

Interior of the Avery Coonley House, with hip ceiling. Riverside, Illinois, 1908.

Hardy House, and the prototype 'A Fireproof Home for $5,000', published in 1905 in *The Ladies' Home Journal*.

Wright later wrote of these Prairie Houses, 'Taking a human being as my "scale", I brought the whole house down in height to fit a normal one – ergo, 5'– 8" tall, say. Believing in no other scale than the human being I broadened the mass out all I possibly could, brought it down into spaciousness.'[23] Wright follows this with the claim that, at 5 feet 8½ inches, he was just a bit above the prototypical height. In fact, Wright was somewhere under 5 feet 7 inches, and his height would be a point of great sensitivity throughout his life.

In his work of this period, Wright believed he had moved past the superficial interpretations of classicism of his Beaux-Arts trained contemporaries, establishing a direct connection with ancient architecture in order to return to first principles. This is indicated in the opening of his essay 'In the Cause of Architecture', which accompanied the first national publication of his collected works in *Architectural Record* in 1908:

> Radical though it may be, the work here illustrated is dedicated to a cause conservative in the best sense of the word. At no point does it involve denial of the elemental law and order inherent in all great architecture; rather it is a declaration of love for the spirit of that law and order and a reverential recognition of the elements that made its ancient letter in its time vital and beautiful.[24]

In this essay Wright held that his work was inspired by, and tailored to, progressive American democracy; this view was endorsed by Herbert Croly, editor of *Architectural Record,* prominent national leader of the progressive movement and author of *The Promise of American Life* (1909) and *Progressive Democracy* (1914). In what is virtually a paraphrase of Wright's 1908 statement, it was later noted: 'Progressivism, at its heart, was an effort to realize familiar and traditional ideals under novel circumstances.'[25]

Wright's second Hillside Home School, built for his aunts Ellen and Jane in 1902 in the Valley, indicates that Wright would employ in his Prairie Period public buildings the same cruciform-plan geometries he was using in his houses. The primary space of the school is the meeting room at the corner, which is a two-storey space, square in plan, with a mezzanine balcony that is rotated 45 degrees to form a 'rotated square' – a medieval proportioning system used to size the stepped sections of Gothic cathedral towers. On the exterior, the stone piers and walls rise directly from the ground, looking as if they had grown there, and the pyramidal wooden roof and window mullions interlock with these walls so that the building is strongly anchored to both the earth and the sky.

For the enlightened clients of the Larkin Company of 1902, Elbert Hubbard, an early exponent of the dignity of labour and

The Larkin Building, Buffalo, New York, 1902. View of the interior, looking into the central court from the top, dining-room floor.

founder of the Roycrofters, an Arts and Crafts-inspired movement, John Larkin, William Heath and company president Darwin Martin, Wright was able to create a truly humane workplace as a prototype for American business. A critique of Chicago skyscrapers, Wright's Larkin Building was organized around a central interior court, which was naturally illuminated by skylights, with large windows in the workspaces set high in the outer walls so that the workers were given views of the sky, and not of the industrial context. The result, which Wright called 'a simple cliff of brick', a 'protestant' against the typical emphasis on appearance over substance in public buildings, was designed to be perceived at eye-level on the ground. This is indicated by Wright's sharply critical reaction to the national publication of photographs taken from a height several floors up, part of a review by a writer who had never even visited the building in person.[26]

Among the humane aspects of the Larkin Building were the natural lighting and air-conditioning (the first in the US) of the office spaces; the removal of the services and stairs to the outer corners of the building, where they were organized in towers, allowing all the workspaces to open to the central interior court; the first employment of built-in filing cabinets; the first wall-hung toilets and partitions, and cantilevered desk chairs, all to expedite cleaning; a branch library and social spaces for the workers; and the 'upside down' organization that placed the company officers on the ground floor, overlooked by the workers above. Particularly notable was the top-floor dining room with dining tables designed by Wright so that a chair could not be placed at the 'head' of the table, requiring officers and staff to sit as equals. Taking their cue from the inspirational phrases Wright had carved into the walls at the top of the central court, the management of the Larkin Company had an organ installed in the central space to provide music for the employees, and readings of Emerson were given during work breaks.

In Unity Temple (1905), arguably his greatest work of the Prairie Period, Wright created an entirely new expression for liberal religious space, at once entirely modern yet also ancient in feeling. Designed for the congregation of which he was a member, and engaging his deep understanding of Unitarianism, Wright achieved a complete integration of material and space, a unity of place and experience. Built by Paul Mueller, as were all Wright's major buildings of the period, including the Martin House and the Larkin Building, Unity Temple was the first exposed, reinforced cast concrete public building in America, built on and of the rock of the earth – a true 'rock-built' temple, as Wright's uncle Jenkin Lloyd Jones described it.

Grounding Unity Temple in the long tradition of centralized sanctuaries and temples, rather than in the recent tradition of

Unity Temple,
Oak Park, Illinois,
1905, interior.

steeple-topped churches, Wright constructed a top-lit central sanctuary, in plan a square interwoven with a cruciform so as to form
four shallow balconies at the outer edges. The central room is supported by four massive square piers, which carry both structural
loads and heated air, behind which four stairways are housed in
the outer corners, and the ceiling of the sanctuary is opened with
25 amber-coloured skylights, to allow the room to be flooded with
warm light even on the greyest winter day. In entering, one makes
seven turns, passing through low dark passages before finally arriving in the tall, brightly lit sanctuary, which seats four hundred in a
space at once intimate and monumental, and which inspires the
discussion among recognizable neighbours typical of the Unitarian

Portrait of
Catherine Tobin
Wright and Robert
Llewelyn Wright,
c. 1907.

mode of worship. Wright called the result a noble form, inspired
by his poetic mentor, Whitman: 'Chanting the square deific . . .
Out of the old and new, out of the square entirely divine, Solid,
four-sided, all sides needed.'[27]

In the only instance of its kind, Wright recorded the design
process for Unity Temple, the primary elements of which he worked
out alone, at night, after the office had closed at 9.00 pm. In his
search for perfection in this most important design, Wright wrote:

> The ideal of organic architecture is severe discipline for the
> imagination. I came to know that full well . . . How many
> schemes I have thrown away because some minor feature
> would not come true to form! . . . These studies never seem to
> end, and in this sense no organic building may ever be "finished".
> The complete goal of the ideal of organic architecture is never
> reached. Nor need be. What worthwhile ideal is ever reached?[28]

The strain on Wright of the endless hours and ever higher ideals had begun to show early in this period. In his lecture to the Architectural League in 1900, he had argued that it was patently unfair that the conscientious architect should 'see his wife and children suffer for ideals that may seem ridiculous and are to the average mind incomprehensible.'[29]

In 1903, the same year as the birth of his son Llewelyn, his sixth child, Wright had designed a house for Edwin and Mamah Cheney, and at some point fairly soon after that Wright began an affair with Mamah Borthwick Cheney. She was two years younger than Wright, had a bachelors degree in arts from the University of Michigan, and was enrolled at the University of Chicago. She read widely and was involved in translations of the writings of the Swedish feminist Ellen Key. She was also a member of the Nineteenth Century Women's Club, where she met Grace Hemingway, Ernest's mother, and became close friends with Catherine Wright. Looking back, John Lloyd Wright blamed his father's affair in part on Wright's new automobile, a yellow Stoddard Dayton roadster with a body custom-designed by Wright; after 1905 Wright and Mamah Cheney were often seen driving about together at all hours.[30]

The commission for Unity Temple came immediately after the Wrights had returned from their first trip to Japan, from March to May 1905. Though Wright would later say it was to recover from the effort of the Larkin Building and Martin House, the trip had actually been the idea of Mr and Mrs Ward Willits, clients for one of Wright's greatest Prairie Houses in 1902, who hoped it would allow the Wrights the opportunity to repair their marriage. The Willits, however, returned early after Mrs Willits discovered that Wright had taken her husband to a traditional bath house, staffed by young women.[31] While in Japan Wright travelled extensively, visiting numerous sites including the temple complexes at Nikko, and the bi-nuclear plans of these temples would directly inspire the plan of Unity Temple. Wright took numerous photographs of temples and also of landscapes, gardens and waterfalls, showing a remarkably well-developed understanding of Japanese architecture and garden design.

During this trip Wright also began in earnest what can only be called his lifelong addiction to Japanese woodblock prints, particularly the work of Hiroshige and Hokusai, which he purchased in large numbers. Upon his return from Japan, Wright twice exhibited his Japanese prints at the Art Institute. In March 1906 he exhibited hundreds of prints by Hiroshige, the world's first retrospective of that artist's works. Then, in the 1908 exhibit, Wright not only contributed 218 of the 655 prints shown (the largest exhibition of Japanese woodblock prints ever held in America) but he also designed the exhibit layout, print stands and wall-hanging structures.[32]

Following his father's death in 1904 and his uncle James's death in 1907, Wright grew more and more restless with his life in Oak Park, writing later: 'This absorbing, consuming phase of my experience as an architect ended ... I was losing grip on my work and even interest in it . . . Everything, personal and otherwise, bore down heavily on me. Domesticity most of all. What I wanted I did not know. I loved my children. I loved my home.'[33] In 1908 Wright was visited by Kuno Francke, a German-born professor at Harvard, who told Wright that he was not appreciated in America and that he should go to Europe, where his designs would prove inspirational to the new generation. A short while later Wright received an invitation from the German publisher Ernst Wasmuth to come to Berlin and publish his work. When the Ashbees visited in December 1908 they immediately sensed that the Wrights' marriage was in deep trouble, and they invited both the Wrights to Europe.

Wright asked Catherine for a divorce in 1908, and she said she would grant it if he waited a year, but in 1909 she refused. Wright immediately set about the process of closing his office, arranging to hand over the practice to Herman Von Holst, an astute businessman but mediocre designer, with the understanding that Von Holst should continue to employ Wright's assistants Mahony and Griffin. Wright took this decision despite the fact that, at that very moment, he was completing the design of a house for Harold McCormick, heir to the inventor of the cotton harvester, and his wife Edith, daughter of John D. Rockefeller, and he had recently been commissioned by the automobile inventor and manufacturer Henry Ford to design a large family estate. Van Bergen recalled, only days before Wright was to leave, 'the visit [to the Studio] of Henry Ford and Wright's inability to maintain his customary self-confident manner'.[34] As a result of his abrupt departure, no building by Wright was ever realized for either of these two important American industrialists, and Wright's later experiences with the Rockefeller family would be no more positive. On 20 September 1909 Wright left Oak Park, sailing for Europe the next month.

5

Europe and the Shining Brow
1909–19

Wright's next ten years, often called 'the lost years', began not only with his thriving practice abruptly closed but also with his reputation ruined, for Wright did not go to Europe alone. In New York Wright was joined by his lover Mamah Cheney, who had abandoned her husband and children. After several weeks at the Plaza Hotel, they sailed for London in October 1909. The dramatic change in Wright's career that occurred as a result of his flight to Europe, and the scandal of his and Mamah's affair, is registered in the fact that from 1899 to 1909 he designed 208 projects, of which 114 were built, whereas from late 1909 to 1919 he designed 121 projects, of which 56 were built.[1] Yet to categorize these years as 'lost' is not entirely appropriate, for they would see the commissioning, design and construction of some of Wright's greatest buildings, as well as the introduction of his work to the larger world.

The most important effect of Wright's trip abroad, however, would be on him, since for the first time he visited the great works of European architecture. In Berlin, Wright's initial stop, he was overwhelmed by the early nineteenth-century works of Karl Friedrich Schinkel. Over the next year, in his visits to Vienna, Paris and possibly Amsterdam, Wright closely studied the works of a number of his European contemporaries, including Joseph Hoffmann, Otto Wagner, Hendrik Berlage and Peter Behrens. Wright, after being called 'the Olbrich of America' by the head of Wasmuth, went to Darmstadt to see the artists' colony of

Portrait of Mamah
Borthwick Cheney,
c. 1909.

Matildenhohe designed by Joseph Maria Olbrich, Wright's exact
contemporary, who had passed away in 1908, aged 40. Wright
also visited Olbrich's Secessionist Building in Vienna of 1898,
which had been published in *The Studio*. During Wright's year in
Europe he made repeated visits to Berlin, and in a remarkable
coincidence three other major Modern architects, Walter Gropius,
Ludwig Mies van der Rohe and C. E. Jeanneret, later called Le
Corbusier, were at that time working together in the Berlin office
of Behrens.

Cheney had her own personal agenda in this year abroad. In early 1910 she left Wright in Paris and went to Sweden to meet Ellen Key, who made Cheney her official English-language translator. Over the next two years Cheney, with Wright's assistance, would translate Key's feminist writings, then being widely read in Europe, including *The Morality of Woman*, *Love and Ethics*, *Ibsen and Women* and *The Woman Movement*.[2] During their year in Europe, Cheney also taught languages at the University of Leipzig.

By March 1910 Wright had settled in Florence, where he was joined by Taylor Woolley, one of the last draughtsmen hired at the Oak Park Studio, and Wright's son Lloyd, who at age nineteen had withdrawn from the University of Wisconsin to work with his father on the hundred drawings for the Wasmuth monograph; their expenses were paid by the proceeds of a sale of some of Wright's Japanese prints to Sallie Casey Thayer of Kansas City. They first lived and worked in a small villa called 'Fortuna' located below the Piazzale Michelangelo, to the south across the River Arno from the historic centre of Florence. In late spring, joined by Cheney, they moved to the Villa Belvedere in Fiesole, an ancient town eight kilometres from Florence, a 45-minute trip by the new electric tram, the first of its kind in Europe.[3]

Wright was so happy during his time in Italy that he designed, for a site in Fiesole, a small villa and studio for Cheney and himself; its L-shaped plan presaged his Taliesin of the next year. Another subtle and rarely noticed reference to the two lovers occurs in the Wasmuth portfolio itself, where the forty-second sheet, numbered xxx, depicts, side by side, the plans of the Cheney House and the astonishingly dynamic project titled 'House for an Artist', clearly intended for Wright himself. This is the only instance in the entire portfolio where the plans of two different buildings appear together on one page.

Wright opened his introductory text for the Wasmuth portfolio by stating that, living in Italy, he 'had the privilege of studying the work' of Giotto, Masaccio, Brunelleschi, Bramante, Sansovino and Michelangelo – the great architects and artists of the Italian Renaissance. From his reference to Bramante and Sansovino we know he visited Rome and Venice, in addition to many hours spent in Florence. Wright recalled how he and Cheney, after visiting art galleries such as the Uffizi in Florence, would sit exhausted on the benches, 'saturated with the plastic beauty' of buildings, sculptures and paintings. Wright's descriptions are strikingly similar to those of Henry James, the Boston Unitarian living in England, whose travel writings had been published in 1909 as *Italian Hours*. James praised Fiesole's exceptional views of Florence and the perfect light of the Uffizi's glazed top-floor gallery,[4] descriptions that James had also employed almost verbatim in such novels as *Portrait of a Lady* (1881).

The work on the Wasmuth portfolios completed, Wright started for home in September 1910, travelling first to London, where he met Ashbee. Wright was taken to Chipping Campden in the Cotswolds, to which Ashbee had removed his Guild of Handicraft from the East End of London in 1902. Initially established as a type of settlement house, similar to Toynbee Hall and Hull House, where the arts and crafts were used to improve the conditions in an impoverished neighbourhood, Ashbee's Guild of Handicraft had, in its new rural setting, evolved into a communal enclave where its members both lived and worked. The impact on Wright of this model for a collective craft community, directed by a master artist, was immediate and his conception of his own similar communal guild enclave may be dated from this experience.[5]

While Cheney remained in Germany until she obtained her divorce the next year, Wright sailed for America. He arrived in Oak Park on 8 October 1910, one year after he had left, and was literally welcomed home with open arms by his wife and children. He was not prepared, however, for the intensity of criticism he received, including front page articles in the Chicago papers and Oak Park pastors damning him from their pulpits. At first Wright seemed

Taliesin living room, view towards fireplace. Spring Green, Wisconsin, 1911.

intent upon repairing his reputation, renovating his Oak Park Studio into apartments in order to generate rent to support his wife, and opening an office in Orchestra Hall in downtown Chicago, where his sons Lloyd and John soon joined his practice. However, in 1911 he designed a Studio and Residence for himself on Goethe Street, which, while never realized, clearly indicated his true intentions regarding his wife and family.

Wright's Oak Park life was over, and he now began work on a house and studio near Spring Green, Wisconsin. Initially this was disguised as a project for his mother, Anna, who wanted to return to the Valley to be near her Lloyd Jones relatives. Wright called his house and studio 'Taliesin', the name of an ancient Welsh poet, also meaning 'shining brow'. Taliesin was wrapped around the hill, enclosing the hilltop and its enormous oaks in a loosely defined central court. Wright developed the large multi-function complex as a series of semi-independent pavilions, linked by loggias and woven into the landscape. In a manner markedly different from the Prairie

Houses, the house portion of the complex was asymmetrical, L-shaped in plan, and wrapped around the garden court. Built of stone laid in horizontal layers as it came from the quarry, opened in all directions by bands of casement windows, and sheltered by low, overhanging, cedar-shingled roofs, Taliesin nestled into its hillside site, integrating with the rural landscape as if it had been there forever. Seen from the approach below, Taliesin, as it was first built, looked remarkably like the Dalai Lama's palace of Potala at Lhasa, Tibet, a photograph of which Wright had hung in the drafting room – the only work by another architect ever given this honour.

Overlooking the Wisconsin River valley below, from Taliesin Wright could see his 1896 'Romeo and Juliet' windmill, while over the hill was his 1902 Hillside Home School, and scattered through the neighbouring vales were the farms of his mother's family. It was here in the 'Valley of the God-Almighty Joneses' that he started anew, with Mamah Borthwick (who had reverted to her maiden name after receiving her divorce) joining him in autumn 1911. Young architects were again drawn to Wright, despite his remote refuge, to work in the first Taliesin's remarkably intimate drafting room, scaled to the seated figure, with natural light entering from four sides. Built works from this early period at Taliesin include the Herbert Angster House, the Avery Coonley Playhouse, the Banff National Park Recreation Building in Canada, the Lake Geneva Inn, the Francis Little House and a house for his mother in Spring Green.

Wright also continued his earlier evolution of new prototypes for both middle-class housing and suburbs, building on his Como Orchards project of 1908 and his Bitter Root Town plan of 1909 with a series of projects for Sherman Booth in Glencoe, Illinois, first designed in 1911 but not realized until 1915. In 1913, in response to a competition sponsored by the Chicago City Club, Wright designed the 'Model Quarter Section for City Residential Land Development', in which public, commercial, institutional and cultural buildings were woven together, through a series of parks, with private housing structured in the pinwheel 'quadruple block' configuration Wright had first envisioned in 1900. Intended as a place where American democracy could flourish, this community of six thousand residents was an urban 'quarter' in which one could live, work, shop, attend cultural and sports events, and where the entire neighbourhood was within a ten-minute walking distance – all ideas that have recently been presented as 'new urbanism', without any credit to Wright.

Wright had ended his 1910 Wasmuth text by acknowledging his 'debt to Japanese ideals', and in 1912 he published *The Japanese Print: An Interpretation*, which, despite its title, is the most comprehensive revelation ever made by Wright of his own fundamental design principles. In this little-studied text, Wright held that aesthetics and ethics were one and the same, 'abstractions' simultaneously good and beautiful; called for a 'disciplined power to see' in order to move beyond the surface effects of the 'literal, objective, realistic, and therefore unreal'; and stated, 'Geometry is the grammar, so to speak, of the form. It is its architectural principle.'[6]

At this moment it seemed Wright's fascination with Japanese culture might have the opportunity to move beyond the collecting of prints. In 1911 the Chicago banker Frederick Gookin, one of the country's foremost experts on Japanese prints, and co-contributor with Wright to the 1908 Art Institute Exhibit, recommended Wright for the Imperial Hotel commission in Tokyo. From January to May 1913 Wright and Borthwick went to Japan in the hope of securing the commission, and to purchase more woodblock prints. Another economic recession began in 1913, and while Wright was receiving commissions during this period, they never generated enough revenue to cover the expenses at Taliesin or his trips abroad. Wright turned to his client and friend Darwin Martin, one of the highest-paid executives in America when he first hired Wright, for a series of loans, usually secured against Japanese prints from Wright's collection.

In 1913 Wright was commissioned by Edward Waller Jr (son of the Waller in whose house Burnham's offer was made) to design Midway Gardens, a place for public entertainment and dining in Chicago. Wright recalled Waller saying, 'I want to put a garden in this wilderness of smoky dens, car-tracks and saloons', and Wright responded with one of his greatest works, a fusion of landscape and architecture. The structure was built by Paul Mueller on a site 90 m (300 ft) square, with the indoor 'winter garden' along the main street to the east, and the major volume, the outdoor 'summer garden', a series of landscaped and paved garden terraces stepping down towards the bandstand at the west end of the site. In Midway Gardens Wright intended to 'weave a masonry fabric' of brick, terracotta tiles and site-cast concrete blocks and coloured trim, resulting in his most complete 'total work of art', which included designs for sculpture, furniture, lighting fixtures, dishware, decorative patterns and details, many executed with the help of craftsmen Richard Bock and Alfonso Ianelli.

Designed and built in an astonishing nine months, the opening of the still-unfinished Midway Gardens on 27 July 1914 was, as Wright recalled, 'as brilliant a social event as Chicago ever knew', and the acoustics of the outdoor bandstand at the end of the summer garden were pronounced 'perfect' – proof of Wright's training with Adler. Each weekend that summer more than 17,000 people paid admission to attend performances of music by the National Symphony, of dance by the Russian Anna Pavlova, and to take meals in Midway Gardens.[7] Wright wrote later, 'In a scene unforgettable to all who attended, the architectural scheme of color, form, light, and sound came alive with thousands of beautifully dressed women and tuxedoed men. The scene came upon the beholders as a magic spell. All moved and spoke as if in a dream.'[8]

Wright's dream was brutally shattered soon afterwards. On Saturday 15 August, shortly after the First World War had begun, Wright was taking lunch as his son John painted a mural at the

Midway construction site when word came of a terrible tragedy at Taliesin – fire and murder. They took the first train to Spring Green, on board meeting Edwin Cheney as well as a group of reporters, from whom Wright apparently first learned the full story. A deranged servant had bolted the doors of the dining room shut, set fire to the house and killed the occupants with a hatchet. Mamah Borthwick, her two children and four others were murdered, and the domestic portion of Taliesin was burned to the ground. 'She for whom Taliesin had first taken form . . . gone,' he later wrote, and it was a blow from which the 47-year-old Wright never fully recovered.

But for Wright 'there is release from anguish in action': he rebuilt Taliesin even larger than before, burying himself in his work. His wife Catherine continued to hope for a reconciliation, but it was not to be. In late 1914 Wright met Miriam Noel, a 45-year-old widow, daughter of a prominent plantation and slave-owner in Tennessee, accomplished artist and collector of art who had been living in Paris at the outbreak of the war; unknown to Wright, she was also a morphine addict. Noel came into Wright's life in his moment of greatest need, and only afterwards did her own deeply troubled and dependent nature slowly emerge. Over the next dozen years they would have a tempestuous, on-again, off-again romance that Wright described from its start as an 'entanglement'.

It was during this tragic period that Wright in 1914 published his second essay in *Architectural Record*, again entitled 'In the Cause of Architecture', in which he berated his former Oak Park associates for using his forms: 'The style of the thing, therefore, will be the man – it is his. *Let his forms alone.*' Yet, in a perceptive assessment of his achievements to date, Wright noted: 'Were no more to come of my work than is evident at present, the architecture of the country would have received an impetus that will finally resolve itself into good.'[9] Indeed, just as the Columbian Exposition may be seen as the provocation that helped bring the Chicago School into existence in 1893, Wright's closing of his Oak Park Studio resulted in the blossoming of the Prairie School. Wright's former apprentices were now out on their own, out from under his considerable shadow, and his influence spread even as he criticized the results.

Meanwhile, at Taliesin Wright was at work on a number of commissions that reflected the change in character in his designs resulting from his recent studies of earlier indigenous American architecture, the Pre-Columbian structures of Mesoamerica. Wright had seen the full-scale reconstructions of Maya temples at the 1893 Columbian Exposition, and in 1915 his sculptor associate Alfonso Ianelli had accompanied him to see the detailed architectural models of Maya temples at the Panama-California Exposition in San Diego.[10] This heavier, more massive character was first seen in the designs, all unrealized, for a theatre for Aline Barnsdall, whom Wright had first met in 1915; the Christian Catholic Church; the Carnegie Library; the Kehl Dance Academy; and the Spaulding Print Gallery in Boston for America's premier collectors of Japanese prints. Works exhibiting this new character that were built include the A. D. German Warehouse, in his home town of Richland Center, and residences for Emil Bach, Henry Allen and Frederick Bogk.

Wright's most intriguing and extensive designs of this period were the 'American Ready-Cut System' houses for the Richards Company of Milwaukee, documented in a thousand drawings, and comprising dozens of prototypes for a wide variety of freestanding suburban houses, townhouses, attached duplexes, urban rowhouses and apartment buildings. All were intended for middle-class American families, with their modular components to be mass-produced by factory prefabrication, and a number of these designs were built.

During this period a number of new apprentices arrived to work with Wright, particularly from Europe and Japan, where Wright's reputation was growing rapidly. Among these were Antonin

Raymond, a Czech émigré who arrived with his wife Noemi in the spring of 1916, Arato Endo from Japan and Rudolph Schindler, an Austrian émigré who came in early 1918. Most of these architects came to work on the Imperial Hotel commission, which Wright received officially during a visit to Taliesin in February 1916 by Aisaku Hayashi, manager of the Imperial Hotel. From 1916 to 1922 Wright would make multiple trips to Japan, where in addition to the Imperial he was also commissioned to design a number of houses and public buildings, most of which were realized.

In early 1917 it became clear that the US was moving towards entering what would later be called the First World War, on the side of Britain. True to his progressive roots, Wright was a passionate pacifist, an early isolationist who bitterly opposed the war. In this he was far from alone, for many Americans who considered themselves part of the Progressive movement felt betrayed by their fellow progressive President Woodrow Wilson's change from his original policy of neutrality. Wright's British friend Ashbee tried to reason with Wright, but Wright believed that the war was the result of British imperialism and his deep sympathies for Germany, the foreign country that had first recognized his genius, were genuine. This was despite the fact that Elbert Hubbard, Wright's friend, Larkin client and founder of the Roycrofters, had gone down with the *Lusitania* when it was sunk by a German submarine in 1915.

The Unitarian Lloyd Jones clan, pacifists all, stood firmly against the war, and the 72-year-old Jenkin Lloyd Jones and his wife, along with Jane Addams and many others, were aboard Henry Ford's famous 'peace ship' in 1915 when it sailed to Europe to campaign for an arbitrated ending to the war. Upon their return, Jones was asked what he thought they had accomplished. Stroking his long white beard, Jones replied, 'We made a deep impression on the neutral countries.'[11] Wright's and his uncle's continued opposition to American involvement in the war brought severe criticism, resulting in Wright being investigated by the FBI and Jones's journal *Unity* being banned from the US mail. Jenkin Lloyd Jones had just managed to get the ban removed when he passed away in September 1918, two months before the armistice.[12]

It was at this same time that Sullivan, who had seen a steady decline in his practice since the ending of his partnership with Adler in 1895, and who was then completing a series of elegant small town banks across the Mid-West, made a telephone call to Wright at Taliesin. While it appears they had spoken occasionally since their break in 1893, starting as early as 1900, when Ashbee recalls being introduced to Sullivan by Wright, it was only after 1918 that Wright and Sullivan would again become close.

It has been pointed out that Wright was the only great Modern architect not traumatized by the First World War, an event that dramatically changed the nature of European Modernism in all the arts.[13] However, Wright's personal tragedy at Taliesin, occurring almost exactly at the moment the war began, acted to change his world view, marking the beginning of his slow but steady withdrawal from urban society, and his increasingly negative attitude towards the city and the economic forces that controlled and shaped it.

In a lecture entitled 'Chicago Culture', given to the Women's Aid Organization in 1918, Wright both championed and critiqued Chicago, which he called 'the national capital of the essentially American spirit', arguing that the city was the last and only hope for democracy, and for a democratic culture in America. In this extraordinary lecture, Wright also situated 'his highly personal and innovative achievements in the larger context of the culture where he lived and worked.'[14] Paraphrasing the Chicago sociologist Robert Park, Wright noted that, 'In a great workshop like Chicago this creative power germinates . . . the seeds of a genuine culture.' Wright then listed those who have been part of this germination of culture, including architects Louis Sullivan and John Wellborn

Root, landscape architect Jen Jensen, Harriet Monroe, the founder of *Poetry* magazine, social critic Thorstein Veblen, writers George Ade, Hamlin Garland and Ring Lardner, attorney Clarence Darrow (who would in 1925 argue for the right to teach evolution in Chicago's famous Scopes trial), religious leaders (whom Wright calls 'sky pilots') Bishop Cheney, Rabbi Hirsch and Reverend Jenkin Lloyd Jones, educators Francis Parker and John Dewey, leaders of the 'new theater' movement Donald Robertson and Maurice Brown, and artists Jerome Blum, Pauline Parker, Charles Francis Browne and Lorado Taft.

After noting that the Art Institute of Chicago is the 'largest and most successful in point of attendance of any institution of art in America', Wright launched a scathing critique of the consumer 'culture', focused on fashion, which Chicago, 'born in a swamp' and 'chief butcher shop of the world', had 'bought and borrowed . . . ready-made'. Arguing that 'culture comes through *being* not *buying*' (a fundamental concept he shared with Dewey), Wright stated that, 'if democracy means anything at all . . . it means easier, surer recognition of the qualities of the individual' over the mediocrity of 'the fashionable thing [which] is valueless to culture'.[15] In this penetrating critique of Chicago's materialistic and economic success and its concomitant ethical and aesthetic failure, Wright anticipates John Dos Passos's great trilogy of novels, *USA*, which would not be published until more than a decade later.

6

Eastern Garden and Western Desert
1919–29

In one of the longest sections of *An Autobiography*, Wright recalls
the almost four years that he lived in Japan, from 1919 to 1922,
working on the Imperial Hotel in Tokyo.[1] While Wright worked his
usual long hours in the drafting room, he also walked through the
city nearly every day, as well as taking longer trips to the countryside and other cities on weekends. He immersed himself in
Japanese daily life, wearing a kimono at home and at the inns he
visited while travelling. 'The Japanese house fascinated me and I
would spend many hours taking it to pieces and putting it back
together again,' Wright wrote, using language he had previously
only employed in describing his own Unity Temple. In the houses
he visited, he studied the modular *tatami* mats, roughly three feet
by six feet, that served to organize the plan; the heated floors, a
concept brought from Korea; and the way that the house and garden
were interwoven, so that one could not tell where one ended and
the other began. Wright engaged in the tea ceremony, studying its
rituals, as defined by Rikkyu, and the underlying philosophy of
Lao Tzu, in *The Book of Tea* by Okakura Kakuzo, author of the
Columbian Exposition pamphlet on the Ho-o-den. Although written
in 1906, Wright first read *The Book of Tea* after he received a copy
as a gift from his Imperial Hotel client, Baron Okura.

'The pursuit of the Japanese print became my constant recreation while in Tokyo. A never-failing avocation . . . Some said
obsession,' Wright wrote, 'the print is more autobiographical than

you may imagine. If Japanese prints were to be deducted from my education I don't know what direction the whole might have taken.' It was during this period, and with the generous fees paid by the Imperial Hotel, that Wright dramatically enlarged his collection of Japanese prints. His son John later wrote that Wright 'was buying so many works of oriental art that vendors poured in every day and stood in line in the lobby of the hotel from morning until night. It kept him jumping from his stool at the drafting board to examine these antiques as they were presented to him.'[2] Wright was also buying large numbers of prints for the major collectors in America, such as John and William Spaulding of Boston, whose collection was later donated to the Boston Museum of Fine Arts, Howard Mansfield, buyer for the Metropolitan Museum of New York, Sallie Thayer of Kansas City, whose collection was later donated to the Spenser Museum, and Frederick Gookin, buyer for the Art Institute in Chicago. After his return to the US, Wright could rightly claim that, of the prints, 'America owns the finest collections in the world', largely due to his own voracious purchasing during this time.

Wright and Noel lived in a spacious apartment complete with a fireplace ('fire always burning') and a grand piano, located in the hotel's temporary annex, which had been designed by Wright and built in 1919. Above, on the roof, was a studio and bedroom penthouse, where, as Wright wrote, 'I could work, disturbing no one, and could tumble into bed when tired out.' Joining Wright from Taliesin were Arato Endo, Antonin Raymond, Wright's son John, and the engineer and builder Paul Mueller, all of whom brought their wives. In addition Wright was given a large atelier of young Japanese draughtsmen, most being recent graduates from the University of Tokyo, who laboured to produce the more than 700 drawings for the hotel.

The Imperial Hotel is closely related to the design of Midway Gardens, with two long wings of rooms framing a central garden

Architects in front of the Imperial Hotel, Tokyo. Frank Lloyd Wright is on the far left wearing a white helmet, behind him stands Arato Endo, and to their right, in white, is Paul Mueller.

space in which were placed the public rooms, including the lobby, dining room, theatre (complete with revolving stage – an idea Wright had earlier found in Japanese *kabuki* theatre), ballroom, cabaret, the whole united by a promenade. Wright wrote that his design was not the imposition on the Japanese people of an outside 'Modern' or American architecture, but was intended as a homage to 'Japan the Modern Ancient', to the tradition of the Japanese house, temple and garden: 'The Imperial Hotel is designed as a system of gardens and sunken gardens and loggias that are also gardens – and roofs that are gardens – until the whole arrangement becomes an interpenetration of gardens. Japan is Garden-land.'[3]

Wright wrote that 'the fear of the temblor never left me while I planned the building', Tokyo being in one of the zones of highest seismic activity in the world. Every aspect of Wright's design was informed by this fact, starting with his proposal to float the building on 60 feet (18.3 m) of soft soil, constructing a shallow foundation consisting of thousands of concrete 'pins' nine inches (228 mm) in diameter and eight feet (2.45 m) deep, two feet (610 mm) on centre, the whole bound together with a thick mat slab of reinforced concrete at grade. Wright also developed a cantilevered system for supporting the floor loads, 'as a waiter carries his tray on upraised arm and fingers at the center – *balancing* the load.' Both were untried innovations in Japan, and, though they were directly derived from practices long standard in Chicago (developed first by Jenney and Adler, respectively), Wright's design was initially doubted even by his own engineer, Paul Mueller. As a final protection against earthquakes, Wright divided the building into a series of separate parts, each no longer than 60 feet, with joints running from roof to foundation – 'a jointed monolith with a mosaic surface of lava and brick'.

The massive structure, on which 600 workers laboured for four years, was built of double-layered brick exterior walls filled with concrete (a Roman technique, updated by the use of steel reinforcing), trimmed with perforated, shadow-casting terracotta castings and hand-carved local Oya stone, 'a workable light lava weighing as much as green oak', and topped by copper roofs, this last to avoid the deaths by flying ceramic roof tiles typical in earthquakes. So much Oya stone was quarried that, as Wright wrote, the hole in the ground was the size of the excavations for Grand Central Terminal in New York. Complementing the symmetry of the building structure itself, Wright employed asymmetrical compositions in designing almost everything else in the Imperial Hotel, including the wall murals, furniture for the guest rooms (of two types, western and traditional Japanese), dishware, linens and integrated lighting fixtures.

Compared to contemporary public buildings in Europe and the US, the Imperial Hotel was rather dimly lit, and this was indicative of Wright's understanding of the traditional Japanese culture of 'half-light'. In the West the then-emerging Modern movement in architecture, and indeed the entire era starting with the Enlightenment, called for 'more light', as Goethe was supposed to have cried out on his deathbed. On the contrary, Wright believed that light had no meaning without darkness, and that shadow was the realm of experience, saying, 'Shadow itself is of the light.'[4] As defined in Jun'ichiro Tanizaki's book *In Praise of Shadows* (1933), the inhabited world of 'half-light' is made by shadow: 'we find beauty not in the thing itself but in the patterns of shadows, the light and the darkness that one thing against the other creates. Were it not for shadows there would be no beauty.' It is interesting to note that in his book Tanizaki mentions only one building by name – Wright's Imperial Hotel, which 'with its indirect lighting, is on the whole a pleasant place'.[5]

In the summer of 1922, with the Imperial Hotel almost completed, Wright and Noel left to return to the US. His son John, whom Wright fired after John deducted his unpaid salary from the fee he received for one of Wright's several other Japanese commissions, had already returned. Raymond and Endo would remain in Japan, both going on to successful careers, while Wright's son Lloyd and Rudolf Schindler had been working for several years on Wright's commissions in California. His four years in Japan, while yielding one of his greatest works, had had a devastating effect on Wright's American practice. With only three unbuilt projects commissioned, 1919 was the worst year of Wright's entire architectural career and, despite a booming American economy, the following decade was little better. Between 1919 and 1929 only 67 projects were commissioned; of the seventeen that were built, five were for Wright's own homes and practice. Wright's prime years as a practising architect, from age 52 to age 62, were by far the least productive of his entire career.

One of Wright's most important commissions of this period was from Aline Barnsdall, heiress to an oil fortune, unwed mother, and one of the most important participants in the redefinition of the American theatre that took place in the first two decades of the twentieth century. Barnsdall's close associate, the designer Norman Bel-Geddes, described her as 'erratic, unpredictable, contrary, stubborn, generous', and she would prove to be perhaps Wright's most aggravating client.[6] She first met Wright in 1915, when she was operating out of the Fine Arts Building in Chicago, where Wright had designed four shops. Barnsdall commissioned Wright to design the Chicago Little Theater in 1915, to which he responded with a perfect circle-in-square plan, but soon after she moved to California, where she purchased the 14.5-hectare (36-acre) Olive Hill in Los Angeles and commissioned a new series of works from Wright.

Wright's design for Olive Hill retained the existing olive tree orchard and in fact employed its grid as a basis for the location and structural module of the buildings. Barnsdall's large house captured the hilltop within its court, while the theatre, directors' houses and actors' apartments were arrayed around the sides of the hill, with street-front shops and terrace housing along Hollywood Boulevard, anchored at one end with a cinema. The theatre, as in the Imperial Hotel, included a revolving stage, as well as a plan allowing a degree of spatial interaction between actors and audience that was unprecedented in its time. In the end, only the main house, called Hollyhock after the flower that inspired the cast concrete ornament, and two of the directors' houses were realized.

The Hollyhock House, with its long, rectangular, flat-roofed volumes, carved friezes and massive battered walls surrounding the central courtyard, exemplifies the change in character in Wright's work that had occurred during the seven-year period he worked on the Imperial Hotel. An aerial view of the house, drawn in 1921 by Lloyd Wright, is an exact match for the similar view of the Nunnery Quadrangle, a Maya structure at Uxmal, Mexico, seen from atop the neighbouring Pyramid of the Magician. As this view-point of the Hollyhock House cannot be attained from any actual standpoint on the Olive Hill site, it appears that Lloyd employed a photograph of the Nunnery to construct this drawing of the house, indicating his and his father's strong interest in Pre-Columbian architecture as an indigenous ideal.

The Hollyhock House was published by Wright in 1928 and again in 1942 with the claim that it was built of poured concrete, yet the house is actually constructed of wood framing finished with stucco. Throughout his career Wright had endeavoured to relate the spaces and forms of his designs to the structures and materials with which they were made, looking to nature for its perfect fusion of composition and construction. Immediately following the completion of the Hollyhock House, Wright addressed this issue of 'the nature of the materials' – the ethical conflict between the Hollyhock House's monolithic, heavy appearance and its wood-framed, lightweight construction – by returning to a method of integrated construction using concrete he had first proposed in the Harry Brown House project of 1906.

The 'concrete block system' involved casting concrete into custom-designed forms, imparting Wright's geometric patterns to the block surfaces, then weaving the 16-inch (406 mm) square blocks into walls with reinforcing steel rods laid vertically and horizontally in the blocks' cavities, which were then filled with concrete to fuse the fabric together. With this manner of construction, Wright had found a way to give concrete the modular scale and texture necessary for it to be integrated into his 'unit system' of square grid planning, and he now for the first time called himself 'the weaver', as opposed to 'the sculptor'. During 1923 Wright built a series of these concrete block houses in Los Angeles, including the Alice Millard House ('La Miniatura'), the Samuel Freeman House, the Charles Ennis House and the John Storer House.

After Wright and Noel returned to Taliesin in August 1922, tensions between Noel and Wright's mother Anna increased to the point where, in the autumn, Anna felt she had to leave Taliesin. She never returned to live there, passing away in February 1923. Wright's wife Catherine finally granted him a divorce late that year, and in November, despite his misgivings about her continued fits of anger, Wright married Miriam Noel. But this brought no peace to his personal life, and his practice was simultaneously suffering a series of setbacks. Major projects for the Lake Tahoe Summer Colony in California, the Nakoma Country Club in Madison, the Kindergarten and Theater for Barnsdall in Los Angeles, the Odawara Hotel in Japan, and the Doheny Ranch Resort in the Sierra Madre Mountains above Los Angeles, all were stopped short of construction. The Lake Tahoe and Doheny Ranch projects were both victims of the Teapot Dome scandal that rocked the nation's capital that year, in which Wright's client Edward Doheny was one of two oil tycoons to whom national oil reserves were illegally leased by President Warren Harding's Secretary of Interior, in exchange for interest-free loans and campaign contributions to the Republican party.

The Imperial Hotel had been completed in 1923, and in early September the most powerful quake in modern Japanese history hit Tokyo, levelling large portions of the city. Wright had to wait ten days, during which newspapers claimed the Imperial Hotel was destroyed, before he received news in the form of a telegram from Baron Okura: 'Hotel stands undamaged as monument to your genius. Hundreds of homeless provided by perfectly maintained service.'[7] Wright's 'jointed monolith' had held firm, and the pools at the entrance – almost removed in final budget cuts – provided water to stop the fires that destroyed most of the neighbouring buildings. Wright's design was hailed by Louis Sullivan, in an essay written in 1923, as 'the high water mark thus far attained by any modern architect'; in a second essay, written in early 1924 after the quake, he asserted that the Imperial Hotel 'is not an imposition on the Japanese, but a free will contribution to the finest elements of their culture.'[8]

In his essay of 1923, Sullivan referred to another place where foreign architects had produced what he considered the most appropriate design – the 1922 competition for the new building to house the *Chicago Tribune*, the city's premier newspaper. Neither

Interior of Taliesin drafting room, with Richard Neutra in the foreground, Wright to the left rear, *c.* 1925.

Wright nor Sullivan entered designs in the competition, but a number of their former colleagues did, including Walter Burley Griffin, William Drummond, and the firm of William Holabird and Martin Roche. Yet it was the entries from Europe that later received the most attention, including those from Bruno Taut, leader of the German 'Glass Chain', Walter Gropius, director of Weimar Bauhaus, and the Viennese Adolf Loos, author of 'Ornament and Crime' (1910). While the competition was won by the young New York architect Raymond Hood, Sullivan praised as best and most appropriate the second place design by the Finn Eliel Saarinen.

In 1924, at a time when Wright and he had again grown very close, Sullivan passed away. At Sullivan's funeral Wright met the Austrian architect Richard Neutra and his wife Dione, and they soon joined Wright at Taliesin. Already working at Taliesin were the Swiss architect Werner Moser and the Japanese architect

Oglivanna Lazovich Hinzenberg (later Wright) and Iovanna, *c.* 1927.

Kameki Tsuchiura, and the German architect Erich Mendelsohn came to visit Wright that same year. At least partly as a response to the *Chicago Tribune* competition, Wright was at that time engaged in designing the National Insurance Company Building for a site facing the lake on Michigan Avenue in Chicago. This skyscraper was unlike any before it, a true innovation within the Chicago tradition, with its structure cantilevering out from central supports, like the limbs of a tree, and its outer skin a hanging 'curtain wall' of suspended glass and copper screens. Shortly before his death this design was shown to Sullivan, who told Wright, 'I never could have done this building myself, but I believe that, but for me, you could never have done it.'[9]

The client for the Chicago skyscraper was Albert Johnson, who that same year had also commissioned Wright to design a walled compound of dwellings and a chapel for him in Death Valley, the Mojave Desert, California. The impact of the western American desert landscape on Wright was immediate and intense. During the time he was working on the Johnson project Wright designed a little-known desert dwelling for himself. The modest living unit was located at the rear of an octagonal concrete-walled court, shaped like a bowl, open to the sky, shaded by a canvas cover and closed to the desert horizon, a primitive camp carved into the desert floor. None of these designs for the Mojave Desert was ever realized, but the desert would captivate Wright for the rest of his career.

In November 1924, while attending a Chicago performance of the Russian dancer Karsavina with his friend the painter Jerome Blum, Wright met Oglivanna Lazovich Hinzenberg, born in Montenegro, educated in Czarist Russia, and since 1917 a dancer and one of six lead instructors with Georgei Gurdjieff, the founder in 1921 of the Institute for the Harmonious Development of Man in Fontainebleau, outside Paris. Oglivanna was in Chicago seeking a divorce from her architect husband, and Wright and Miriam had been separated for six months. Wright and Oglivanna fell in love, and three months later she and her daughter Svetlana came to live at Taliesin.

Over the next three years Wright and Oglivanna were ceaselessly hounded and harassed by his wife Miriam, and Wright would build only two works, a new low point in his career. Taliesin burned again in April 1925, the fire caused by an electrical short-circuit, and Wright lost a number of tapestries, screens, bronzes and other treasures he had purchased in Japan, worth by his estimation $500,000. His collection of Japanese prints, however, was saved, as it had been stored in the fireproof vault he had built into the drafting room. Wright sued Miriam for divorce in July, and he and Oglivanna had a child, Iovanna, born in December. They repeatedly fled Miriam's attempts to have them arrested, in 1926 going into hiding in Minneapolis, Minnesota, where they were arrested under the Mann Act, passed in 1910 to curtail the trade in prostitutes across state lines, but now used by the FBI to charge Wright and to threaten Oglivanna and her daughters with deportation.

Almost at the same moment, the banks moved to foreclose on Wright's mortgage and take possession of Taliesin. Wright's friends, led by the ever-loyal Darwin Martin, who had recently commissioned his summer home of Graycliff from Wright, responded by creating Frank Lloyd Wright, Incorporated, to purchase Wright's house and all his future designs. Among those who participated were Alfred MacArthur, part of the family that created the MacArthur Foundation (sponsor of the annual American 'Genius Grants'), Ferdinand Schevill, historian at the University of Chicago, the poet Carl Sandburg, Queene Coonley, the interior designer Joseph Urban, Algonquin 'Round Table' author Alexander Woollcott, Philip La Follette, Wright's attorney, future governor of Wisconsin, and son of the presidential candidate and Progressive Party leader Robert La Follette, as well as Wright's sister Jane. Wright was also given informal legal advice by his friend Clarence Darrow.

For the first four months of 1927 Wright and Oglivanna lived in New York City with his sister Maginel Wright Barney, an illustrator of children's books, and in January Wright supervised the forced sale at the Anderson Gallery of hundreds of his precious Japanese prints, valued at $100,000. Although Wright complained about 'marking time in New York, dying a hundred deaths a day on the New York grid-iron', and 'the sameness, the unanimity, the conformity' of the city,[10] it was during this relatively peaceful time that he wrote the extraordinary series of fourteen essays, entitled 'In the Cause of Architecture', that was commissioned in 1926 by M. A. Mikkelsen, editor of *Architectural Record*, and published from May 1927 to December 1928. He also began writing his autobiography.

While everyone in the US seemed captivated by Wright's personal problems, his renown was growing in Europe. In 1926 Heinrich de Fries published a small monograph on Wright, and in

1925 the Dutch architect H. T. Wijdeveld published a series of special issues of his journal *Wendingen*, collected into a single volume and titled 'The Work of Frank Lloyd Wright', a compilation of his work to date with essays by Wright as well as appreciations by the leading European architects Berlage, J.J.P. Oud, Robert Mallet-Stevens and Mendelsohn, and Sullivan's two essays on the Imperial Hotel. In addition there was an article by the young American writer and critic Lewis Mumford, called 'The Social Background of Frank Lloyd Wright'.

Mumford's essay, written less than a year after the publication of his seminal *Sticks and Stones*, began by tracing the American response to European influence, from the 'churlishness' of Mark Twain's *Innocents Abroad* (1869) to the 'humility' and meek acceptance depicted in Henry James's *The American* (1877). Mumford wrote that contemporary architects seemed faced with a choice: either reject modern technology altogether in a pursuit of traditional form, or model art and life exactly on the processes of the industrial revolution and the machine – in this last Mumford directly cited the work of Le Corbusier. Mumford argued that Wright, in his concern to restore 'man to the central position', in his bringing science and poetry together again, and in his organic integration of architecture and life, was 'an outcast' from both groups, and that his work pointed to a new synthesis: 'Wright has created a true regional form.'[11]

Mumford, with whom Wright first corresponded in 1926, and whom he met while staying in New York the next year, would serve as a link for Wright to the emerging regional architecture and planning movement, an outgrowth of the progressives, which included such figures as Thorstein Veblen, John Dewey, Herbert Croly, Wright's former editor at *Architectural Record* and founding editor of *The New Republic*, Catherine Bauer, author of the seminal *Modern Housing* (1934), and Jane Addams, chair of the Public Housing Association of Illinois, among others. As can be seen in

Wright and family in a motorcar in front of the Ocatillo desert camp, 1929.

his description of Wright's work as 'regional', Mumford had developed the conception of regionalism in architecture far in advance of its much publicized 'rediscovery' following the Second World War.

In late 1927 Wright received a commission from his former Oak Park associate, Albert McArthur, to assist him and his brothers on the Arizona Biltmore Hotel in Phoenix, where they wished to employ Wright's concrete block system of construction. In early 1928 Wright worked in Phoenix, where he met Alexander Chandler, after whom the town of Chandler, Arizona, is named and who commissioned a series of projects for a large resort to be called San-Marcos-in-the-Desert. The next winter Wright, who, now aged 61, was feeling the bite of the bitter Wisconsin winters, moved his office to Chandler, building a desert camp in which to live with his family and work on these projects with his apprentices, including Heinrich Klumb, Donald Walker, Vladimir Karfik, Herbert Fritz,

Interior of Ocatillo, with John Lloyd Wright playing the piano.

Cyrus Adler, George Kastner, Will Weston and his son John, whom Wright had recently asked to return to work seven years after 'firing' him in Tokyo.

Called 'Ocatillo' (variously spelled) by Wright, after the ocotillo cactus, the temporary camp consisted of fifteen pavilions set around the crown of a low desert hill, joined together by a board and batten wall that stepped up and down with the contours of the land, taking their forms from the 30- and 60-degree angles of the surrounding mountains. The roofs were stretched canvas panels, and the apertures were all fitted with hinged canvas flaps operated with ship-rigging cords, so that the building could breathe. A photograph, probably taken by Wright during the brief existence of Ocatillo, shows John Lloyd Wright playing a grand piano, surrounded by Navaho weavings on the furniture and floor, with a telephone prominently displayed on the table, the whole scene bathed in the golden sunlight filtering through the inclined canvas planes overhead.

Wright's remarkably generous and caring personality is evidenced by a story from this time told by the Revd Joseph Vaughan, who in 1929 visited a hospital in Phoenix: 'As I entered the cabin, a distinguished looking gentleman in cardigan jacket and knickers welcomed me. A young man named Sullivan was lying on the bed.' Francis Sullivan, an apprentice who had worked on and off with Wright since 1916, and whom Wright had brought to Arizona in hopes of aiding his failing health, had collapsed that morning. Vaughan continued, 'Only later that night did it occur to me that the good Samaritan was the internationally famous architect Frank Lloyd Wright. When I returned the next morning, Mr Wright was still hovering over the bed as if the dying man were his own son', not leaving Sullivan's side until he passed away.[12]

In the summer of 1927 Wright had finally received a divorce from Miriam, and on 25 August 1928 Wright and Oglivanna were married in a garden in Rancho Santa Fe, California. Things were looking up for Wright in his practice as well, with the numerous projects for San-Marcos-in-the-Desert, the concrete block house for his cousin Richard Lloyd Jones in Tulsa, Oklahoma, and the extraordinary Steel Cathedral commissioned in 1926 by Revd William Norman Guthrie, an Episcopalian minister in New York, who had also commissioned the St Marks-in-the-Bouwerie Apartment Tower, to be built next to the church of the same name in New York. As a further sign of his growing international reputation, Wright had been invited to serve as the North American representative, along with European Eliel Saarinen and South American Horacio Acosta y Lara, on the jury of the design competition for the Christopher Columbus Memorial Lighthouse to be built in Santo Domingo, Dominican Republic.

But there were also other, more unsettling events at this time, such as the demolition in 1929 of Midway Gardens, one of many businesses broken by Prohibition and never able to recover. Wright reacted angrily to the publication of glowing reviews of Le Corbusier's *Towards a New Architecture*, noting how ironic it was that Americans seemed only able to accept new Modern forms –

first conceived in Chicago 25 years before – when they came from Europeans.[13] Wright found himself marginalized by both sides of the debate, with Henry-Russell Hitchcock classing him in *Modern Architecture: Romanticism and Reintegration* (1929) as a 'New Traditionalist', as opposed to Le Corbusier who was called a 'New Pioneer'; and Fiske Kimball, in his *American Architecture* (1928), defending the classicists and consigning Wright to the section titled 'Counter-Currents', prompting Wright to paraphrase Mark Twain in feeling 'the reports of my own death greatly exaggerated'.[14]

These assessments reflected the fact that Wright had spent the entire decade of the 1920s – a ten-year spending spree in the US depicted in F. Scott Fitzgerald's *The Great Gatsby* and Theodore Dreiser's *An American Tragedy*, both published in 1925 – largely on the sidelines. In what most took to be the final devastating blow to Wright's career, none of his designs from the later part of the decade – with the sole exception of his cousin Richard Lloyd Jones's house, built by Paul Mueller – would be realized. On 29 October 1929 the New York Stock Exchange crashed, the start of the Great Depression that brought the nation's economy to a complete halt for the next four years.

Yet in his writings, including his autobiography, which was started during this period, Wright had found another path of influence, and many of his words seem to have been intended not so much for his critics as for young architects, the next generation, such as the then 28-year-old Louis Kahn. In his *Wendingen* text, Wright had noted that 'with all its . . . modernity, the Imperial has the strength of the primitive – it harks back to origins.'[15] And in 1929, in an *Architectural Record* essay attacking Le Corbusier and the International Style, Wright wrote, 'The Modern is. Was always, must always be.'[16]

7

Fellowship and the Disappearing City 1929–39

For Wright the decade from 1929 to 1939 was, at the start, the worst of times, while at the end they would prove – almost miraculously – to be the best of times. When the Great Depression began in 1929 Wright was 62 years old and had been written off by architectural historians and cultural commentators, all of whom assumed that, with the onset of the worst economic crisis in the nation's history, he had retired from active practice, concluding a remarkably successful, virtually unparalleled career of 40 years duration. According to these histories, Wright 'had pointed the way to the promised land that he would never himself enter.'[1] In fact, the five years from 1930 to 1934 would prove to be the nadir of Wright's career, with sixteen buildings commissioned, and only one built. Yet, at this the lowest point of what have been called his 'wilderness years', Wright believed his ideal of 'unfolding' American democracy into architectural form remained unfinished. As his fellow progressive John Dewey wrote at this same time, looking back on his own as yet incomplete efforts: 'Forty years spent wandering in a wilderness like that of the present is not a sad fate, unless one attempts to make himself believe that the wilderness is after all itself the promised land.'[2]

Despite the almost universal assumption that he was finished, it was during the Depression that Wright came to believe himself to be the world's greatest architect, as he stated in an unpublished essay of 1930.[3] This belief was abetted by Wright's friend Alexander

Woollcott, with whom he regularly travelled from New York to Chicago in a Pullman car, who concluded a 1930 article in *The New Yorker* by saying, 'Indeed, if the editor of this journal were so to ration me that I were suffered to apply the word "genius" to only one living American, I would have to save it up for Frank Lloyd Wright.'[4] Wright believed his genius lay in his dignifying and distinguishing of the individual in American democracy, and his architectural vision of daily life taking place in harmony with nature. Wright believed that America, though 'rich beyond the bounds even of our own avarice, living in abundance with creature-comfort undreamed of in the world before', as yet possessed no creative culture.[5] Wright had come to believe 'as few have either before or since, that architecture was a crusading cause on behalf of human civilization rather than a mere profession.'[6]

If he could not build his ideas, Wright could write, lecture and exhibit them. In May 1930 Wright gave six lectures to undergraduate architecture students at Princeton University, sponsored by Otto Hermann Kahn, president of the Metropolitan Opera. *Modern Architecture*, Wright's title for these lectures and the book that followed, was a clear indication of his intention to respond to what was happening in Europe, in particular the International Style (a term it appears Wright coined), and its increasing influence in America. His six lectures called for engaging mechanization and materials with the nature of man; a redefinition of the relationship between design and industrial production; a rejection of mass conformity to fashionable forms in favour of democratic architecture as 'an expression of the dignity and worth of the individual'; an attack on the International Style 'cardboard house' and a championing of the liberative – '*liberal* is the best word' – character of the Prairie Houses; a characterization of the skyscraper as 'space for rent' serving the interests of landowners and not inhabitants; and a scathing critique of Le Corbusier's *Ville Radieuse* for reducing the individual to an anonymous cog in an urban machine that 'extinguishes everyone, distinguishes nothing'. Wright called instead for an architecture 'on the side of *being*', 'in the service of humanity', that would provide 'the background and framework of civilization' – expanding his definition of architecture's task to encompass American culture as a whole.[7]

Wright had been offered eight lectures, but he responded: 'In six days the world was made, and on the seventh the work was visible', proposing instead six lectures and an exhibition to illustrate the principles set forth in the lectures.[8] The exhibit, including more than six hundred photographs and a thousand drawings, with four models, was shown first at Princeton, then in New York at the offices of the Architectural League, followed by Chicago, Madison and Milwaukee. The exhibit then travelled to Europe in 1931, where it was shown in Amsterdam, Berlin, Stuttgart, Antwerp and Brussels with the sponsorship and active support of Wijdeveld, de Fries and Mendelsohn, among others. For the exhibit's European tour, Wright sent his German-speaking senior apprentice, Heinrich Klumb, to coordinate the arrangements and set up the exhibit in each of its venues.

That same year a new World's Fair was being planned in Chicago, titled 'A Century of Progress', and scheduled for 1933, 40 years after the Columbian Exposition. In charge of selecting the architects were Raymond Hood, winner of the 1922 *Chicago Tribune* competition, and Paul Cret, a Beaux-Arts trained professor at the University of Pennsylvania, where he had taught Louis Kahn. Cret recommended Wright's inclusion in the group, but Hood excluded Wright, saying he was incapable of team work. Douglas Haskell protested this decision in *The Nation* and, in *The New Republic*, Mumford stated that '"Hamlet" without the Prince of Denmark could not be a more comical performance' than the Chicago 'Century of Progress' Fair without Wright.[9] Despite these protests in two of the country's great progressive publications, Wright was not included.

In 1931 Wright was invited to participate in a major exhibition at the Museum of Modern Architecture in New York, organized by Philip Johnson and Hitchcock. However, in January 1932 he threatened to withdraw when, as he wrote in a letter to Mumford, he discovered that, having 'consented to join the affair thinking I would be among my peers', hearing only of Le Corbusier and Mies van der Rohe, he found that the exhibit was to include Hood, whom he called the 'eclectic' of both dead and living forms, and Neutra, whom he believed had been trafficking on Wright's name after his nine months at Taliesin.[10] Mumford, saying Wright's absence from the show would be a 'calamity', convinced him to remain. Designed for this 1932 'International Style' exhibition, Wright's 'House on the Mesa' was a regionalist response to the characteristics of its place – the environment, climate, light, material and natural vegetation of the arid setting. Wright's regional, place-specific design served as a pointed critique of the 'universal', placeless characteristics of the International Style that dominated the exhibit.

Despite being written off in the accompanying catalogue by Johnson and Hitchcock as a precursor to the International Style, Wright's publication that same year of *An Autobiography* proved to be of much greater import to his career. Wright's friend Woollcott noted that Wright's writing style was influenced by Carl Sandburg's *Abraham Lincoln, The Prairie Years*, which had been published in 1926, just as Wright began work on his book. Given Wright's friendship with Sandburg and lifelong admiration of Lincoln, this was an entirely appropriate model for Wright's autobiography. Widely and warmly reviewed, *An Autobiography* was a huge success, to be largely credited with the revival of Wright's practice three years later at the end of the economic depression, as well as the powerful hold Wright would exert over the next generation of students in architecture schools – evidenced by one of Louis Kahn's students remarking that 'everyone was carrying a copy [of Wright's book] under their arm' during the ten years Kahn taught at Yale, from 1947 to 1957.

Yet it was also during the period directly after the MoMA International Style exhibition that the European expatriate architects and teachers began to come to the US. Following the closure of the Bauhaus by the Gestapo in 1933, Josef Albers taught at Black Mountain College, started that same year in North Carolina; Walter Gropius was appointed to head the architecture programme at Harvard University in 1938, bringing with him Marcel Breuer and Martin Wagner; and that same year László Moholy-Nagy and Mies van der Rohe came to Chicago to teach. When Mies was appointed director of the Armour Institute (founded in 1893, later renamed the Illinois Institute of Technology), Wright was asked to give an introduction. Recollections vary on what happened next, but most agree that Wright got up before the assembled dignitaries and said, in a pointed reference to Wright's own influence over the development of Modern architecture in Europe, 'I *gave* you Mies van der Rohe', and sat down.

In his *Modern Architecture*, Wright had proposed two constructive solutions to the dilemmas facing the country, calling for industrial design education centres to be founded in rural locations throughout the country, and asserting that American urbanism must inevitably move away from the strangling verticality of the skyscraper as 'space-for-rent' and towards horizontal dispersion of independent landowners across the vast prairie landscape. Wright believed that 'ruralism as distinguished from urbanism is American, and truly democratic'; that decentralization was 'inevitable and desirable'; that it would lead to 'social advantages' over the traditional city – these brought by universal automobile ownership, electronic communication by radio and television, and publication, bringing urban culture to every living room; that 'an acre to the family should be the democratic minimum'; and that 'measured over great free areas, the living interest should be educated to lie in the contact of free individualities in the freedom of the sun, light, and air, breadth of spacing – *with* the ground.'[11]

In these beliefs Wright was hardly alone. Shortly after his death Wright's work and thought were characterized as the culmination of the particularly American tradition of 'the intellectual versus the city' – a tradition that began with Thomas Jefferson's argument for a rural, landowning citizenry, and continued with Emerson, Melville, Nathaniel Hawthorne, Thoreau, Henry Adams, Henry and William James, Frank Norris and Theodore Dreiser.[12] However, a major difference between Wright's concepts and the urban critiques of his contemporaries Addams, Dewey and Mumford, also included in this tradition, was their deep belief in the democratic value of small-scale urban neighbourhoods encouraging face-to-face communication, and Wright's growing faith in the ability of automobile travel and electronic communication to embody democracy among a dispersed population of independent rural households.

Within the progressive movement the end of the traditional city had long been predicted, with Josiah Royce calling for a 'higher provincialism' as the only hope for democracy in 1902, and Frederick Howe writing in 1905 that 'the population must be dispersed'.[13] Henry Ford, in his 1921 proposal for the 120-kilometre (75-mile) long city at Muscle Shoals, Alabama, called for a decentralization of industry and housing 'on the ground', as Wright noted in praising Ford in *Modern Architecture*. Wright's concept, which he called Broadacre City in his book *The Disappearing City* (1932), was also influenced by a number of other sources, including *Fields, Factories and Workshops* (1898) by the anarchist Peter Kropotkin, a Russian prince in exile, who predicted the impact of electrical and communication grids and high-speed motorways leading to the merging of city and country; *Progress and Poverty* (1879) by Henry George, who called for the removal of land from private ownership and the single tax system; and *Anticipations of the Reaction of Mechanical and Scientific Process upon Human Life and Thought* (1901) by H. G. Wells, who predicted the diffusion of the population across the countryside, and their accommodation in what he called the 'practically automatic house'.[14]

Wright's other proposal in his *Modern Architecture* was for an apprenticeship academy, and his vision called for a comprehensive education, based upon the full range of life experiences, similar to a medieval apprenticeship, to take place in nature. During his first trip to Europe in 1909–10 Wright studied Olbrich's artists' colony at Darmstadt as well as Ashbee's Guild of Handcraft at Chipping Campden. He had recently read Mumford's first book, *The Story of Utopias* (1922), and in May 1930 Wright and Olgivanna stayed at his late friend and former client Elbert Hubbard's Roycrofters community at East Aurora, near Buffalo, New York, with his clients the Heaths. During the 1920s Wright was familiar with the Bauhaus at Dessau, an applied arts school with workshops and dormitories housed in a building of Gropius's design. Perhaps the most tantalizing model was his friend Eliel Saarinen's Cranbrook Academy, established in 1929 in Bloomfield Hills, Michigan, with workshops and studios for artists and craftsmen. Also, through his wife Olgivanna, Wright was well aware of Gurdjieff's Institute at Fontainebleau.

In his ideal of education as self-determined, based upon direct experience, Wright's ideas paralleled contemporary developments in higher education, many of them influenced by his friend John Dewey. Two examples with which Wright was familiar were the Experimental College at the University of Wisconsin, Madison, established in 1925 by Alexander Meikeljohn, where Mumford had taught, and the New School for Social Research in New York, founded in 1919 by Dewey, Herbert Croly and Thorstein Veblen. An intriguing parallel development was Black Mountain College, founded in 1933 by John Rice and several others after being dismissed from Rollins College in Florida; this soon included among its faculty Josef and Anni Albers, John Cage, Merce Cunningham, Willem de Kooning, Richard Lippold, Robert Motherwell, Charles Olson and Roger Sessions.

Wright first called his apprenticeship school the Hillside Home School of Applied Arts, and later named it the Taliesin Fellowship. Before it officially opened, Wright offered the position of director to Wijdeveld, who came to Taliesin in 1931 to discuss the position. Wright withdrew the offer upon realizing that his friend 'Dutchy' would not take direction from him; in a letter to Mumford, Wright wrote that Wijdeveld 'makes my egocentricity look like a single color in the spectrum while he has them all. This surprised me. I thought I was the limit.'[15] Mumford declined Wright's subsequent offer to direct the Fellowship, as did Meikeljohn, and Wright decided that he and Oglivanna would act as its directors. In October 1932 the Taliesin Fellowship was begun, funded by the $675 (soon raised to $1,100) tuition Wright required of each apprentice, and by subscriptions from the 'Friends of the Fellowship', which included, among others, the entire writing staff of *The New Yorker*, architects Erich Mendelsohn, Buckminster Fuller, Mies van der Rohe and Albert Kahn, photographers Edward Steichen and Alfred Steiglitz, painter Georgia O'Keeffe, poet Carl Sandburg, orchestra conductor Leopold Stokowski, Albert Einstein and John Dewey.[16]

The Taliesin Fellowship averaged around 25 apprentices, which by 1934 included Elizabeth Bauer (sister of Catherine), Yen Liang, Jack Howe, Willets Burnham (grand-nephew of Daniel), Benny Dombar, William Wesley Peters (soon married to Wright's adopted daughter Svetlana), Edgar Tafel, Bob Mosher, Blaine Drake, Cary Caraway, Elizabeth Kassler, Kay Rattenbury, John Lautner and Eugene Masselink, who in 1933 replaced Karl Jensen as Wright's secretary. Mendel Glickman came soon after as a structures teacher, and he and Peters would be largely responsible for engineering Wright's innovative structures. Several architects who had been with Wright before the Fellowship stayed as senior apprentices, most notably Heinrich Klumb, who was the chief draughtsman. In 1934 Howe took over these duties when Klumb left Taliesin, first working briefly with Louis Kahn, then going on to a successful career in Puerto Rico.

Wright at a table, surrounded by apprentices, among them John Howe, Gene Masselink, William Wesley Peters and John Lautner, *c.* 1935.

For the first several years of the Fellowship the work of the apprentices largely consisted of the substantial renovations and additions necessary to the buildings and landscape of Taliesin, starting with the Hillside Home School that Wright had designed for his aunts in 1902, to which the apprentices added a drafting room surrounded by dormitory rooms. The apprentices, whom Wright called 'volunteers', were not paid for their strenuous work of construction, farming, cooking, cleaning and drafting, leading some of Wright's relatives to remark wryly that he had reinvented slavery. Due to the varied types of work – in the agricultural fields, at the construction site, and at the drafting table, the 'education by example' of the master-architect – as well as the cultural immersion in music, movies, plays and readings, the Fellowship may best be understood as a form of monastic organization, quite close to Wright's medieval model. Yet daily life at Taliesin during the Great Depression was surprisingly modern, as exemplified by the films

The Taliesin drafting room, *c.* 1934.

Wright regularly projected in the theatre newly built within the Hillside School, including those by his personal favourite Sergei Eisenstein, as well as René Clair, Charlie Chaplin and F. W. Murnau.

The only clients for a built work during this dark period were Malcolm and Nancy Willey, who were pleasantly surprised when Wright accepted their commission for a modest middle-class house in Minneapolis. In an indication of the desperation for real work at Taliesin in 1932, as they walked through the Taliesin studio with Wright the Willeys noticed a sign posted on the bulletin board, reading: 'Lo! On the Horizon a Customer Appeareth. By God, He shall not Perish on this Earth.' Wright's amused response was to say, 'I wonder what rascal did that.'[17] In fact, the Willey House, as a prototypical middle-class American house, fits perfectly into the larger plan for Broadacre City that Wright was evolving at that moment. In another striking coincidence, Malcolm Willey had the previous year written a report on regional planning for the President, which proposed linking electronic communication and automobile transportation into a grid to better serve a dispersed population, an idea remarkably close to Wright's Broadacre concept.[18]

Broadacre City, developed directly from Wright's 1913 Chicago City Club Quarter Section competition design, proposed that cultural and commercial spaces be integrated and woven into a continuous landscape fabric of one-acre private dwellings. Conceived in the depths of the Great Depression, at the same moment Franklin Delano Roosevelt's new national government was encouraging subsistence farming, Broadacre City was an agrarian ideal, an agricultural and architectural cultivation of the earth intended to eclipse historical urban culture. Yet it was more than that, for each 10.36-square-kilometre (4 square miles) unit of Broadacre City, based directly upon the grid of the Jeffersonian Louisiana Purchase, was a complete community intended to foster a new kind of local identity through electronic communication and individual mobility, a natural home for a natural economy, ecologically in harmony with the land.

Broadacre City reflects Wright's ideal of relating to the land, based on inhabitation rather than real estate speculation, and of relating to each other – a type of relation possible neither in the density of the traditional city nor in the isolation of rural agrarian life. With this new vision of life in the prairie landscape, Wright also reconnected to Frederick Jackson Turner's 1893 lecture establishing the importance of the frontier and pioneer spirit to American democracy. Wright wrote that 'our pioneer days are not over . . . but the frontier has shifted . . . Pioneering now lies along this new frontier: decentralization.'[19]

For Broadacre City Wright designed every conceivable infrastructure and building type – except for the factory, saying that Albert Kahn's designs could not be bettered. Many of Wright's designs, including in particular what he described as 'spacious landscaped highways, grade crossings eliminated, "by-passing" living areas, devoid of already archaic telegraph and telephone poles and wires and free of blaring bill boards', and surrounded by beautiful parkland,[20] were clearly influenced by his cousin (by marriage)

Robert Moses. Moses, the park director and expressway planner
for New York State profiled in the Pulitzer Prize-winning biography
The Power Broker by Robert Caro, had opened Jones Beach on Long
Island in 1929 and was at that moment completing a system of
automobile parkways linking the new public parks of Long Island
to New York City. Wright and Moses shared a belief in the long-
term beneficial effects of the automobile on the American city,
landscape and way of life; 75 years later this belief has proved to
be far too optimistic.

At that moment Wright met the man who would prove to
be not just a client but a true patron, Edgar J. Kaufmann, owner
of Kaufmann's Department Store in Pittsburgh, Pennsylvania.
Contrary to the myth later created by Kaufmann's son, Edgar
Kaufmann Jr, that it was his enrolment in the Taliesin Fellowship
in October 1934 that brought his father and Wright together, it
appears they had sought each other out at least one year before.
Their pre-existing connections were numerous, including that in
1932 Kaufmann had been asked to support an exhibition of housing at the MoMA by Philip Johnson even as the 'International
Style' exhibit, with Wright's model, was still on display; that the
interior designer Joseph Urban was a close friend of both men;
and that Kaufmann's housing expert Catherine Bauer, Mumford's
lover and sister of Taliesin apprentice Elizabeth, was well known
to Wright. In fact, it appears likely that Kaufmann Jr's enrolment
in the Taliesin Fellowship was his father's idea, and only five days
after his son enrolled Kaufmann offered Wright a series of commissions in Pittsburgh. When they met in November 1934 Wright
asked Kaufmann for funds to help build models of his Broadacre
City concept.[21]

Wright and the Fellowship spent the winter of 1934/5 in
Chandler, Arizona, where Alexander Chandler had commissioned
scaled-down projects. Chandler offered them living and working
quarters at a ranch named La Hacienda, and the central courtyard,

Wright and apprentices around Broadacre City model, courtyard of La Hacienda, Chandler, Arizona, 1934/5.

onto which all the rooms opened, became their studio, where the apprentices constructed a model 3.66 metres (12 ft) square representing four square miles of Broadacre City, as well as models of all the major new building types Wright had conceived for it. The large model was first shown (sponsored by Kaufmann at a cost of more than $7,000) at the 2nd Industrial Arts Exposition of the National Alliance of Art and Industry, which opened in April 1935 in Rockefeller Center in New York.

The Broadacre City model was next exhibited in Washington, DC, at the Corcoran Gallery in July 1935, and Wright sent a letter to President Roosevelt inviting him to attend the opening. Wright had begun cultivating Roosevelt in 1931, sending him a copy of *Modern Architecture* while he was still governor of New York. Roosevelt's 'New Deal' was by this time well under way, if not yet showing much in the way of results. Roosevelt's Resettlement Administration was just constructing its first project, the Jersey Homesteads, designed by Alfred Kastner and Louis Kahn, which involved the relocation of 200 Jewish textile workers and their families from New

York City to Roosevelt, New Jersey. Among those then working in the Resettlement Administration were Frederick Gutheim, one of Mumford's students at Meikeljohn's Experimental College in Madison, where he had spent time at Taliesin with Klumb, as well as no fewer than six former Wright apprentices. It was therefore with some optimism that Wright, in July 1935, met with the director of the Resettlement Administration's Suburban Division to discuss using Broadacre City as a model for a proposed $30 million housing programme. Upon learning that he would have to work within pre-determined guidelines, Wright denounced 'all public and private housing in America' and refused to participate.[22]

That same year Wright had his first serious falling out with Mumford, until now Wright's staunchest defender. Mumford had been architecture critic for *The New Yorker* since 1932. In a review of the New York exhibition of Broadacre City for his 'The Sky Line' column in April 1935, Mumford had, according to Wright, preferred 'the German tenement and slum solution' to Broadacre's 'maximum of space'. Mumford responded that he supported German urban social housing, like Ernst May's Romerstadt in Frankfurt, 'because concentration, when not pushed to the point of congestion, offers certain possibilities of intercourse that dispersion doesn't', and that 'the pattern of Broadacre City too closely resembles that of a con-temporary suburb'.[23] They would not write to each other directly for almost four years. While this disagreement stemmed from Wright's unwillingness to evaluate his house designs separately from their Broadacre City context, it also revealed a far deeper devi-ation in their points of view on the 'minimum existence' house of European functionalism. For Wright, the very concept of a house being designed for a 'minimum existence', rather than a maximum of experience, was against everything in which he believed.

With the commission in 1935 for Kaufmann's country house, called 'Fallingwater', at Bear Run in southwest Pennsylvania, Wright's career began its remarkable recovery. Fallingwater, an

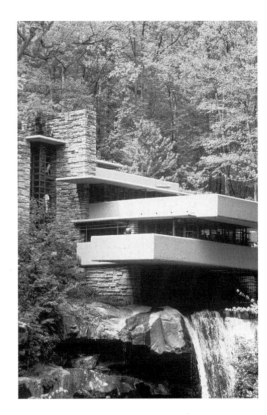

Fallingwater, Bear Run, Pennsylvania, 1935, exterior seen from downstream.

extraordinary and unprecedented series of stone walls supporting concrete terraces and floors cantilevered far out over a mountain stream and waterfall, captured the essence of the fundamental human desire to be at home in the natural world. The stability of the house, its rooted condition, is emphasized and reinforced by the flow of water beneath it, as if it grew from the site, coming out of the ground and into the light. Inspired by the site, but also bringing the character of the natural place into presence – by making it an intimate part of human life – for the first time with his design Wright asserted that when man is 'true to earth his architecture is creative'.[24]

Fallingwater, view from kitchen to cantilevered terrace over waterfall.

While Kaufmann had been expecting Wright to site the house on the south side of the stream, looking north at the waterfall, Wright sited it on the north side of the stream, above the waterfall, with the top of the boulder rising up through the living room floor to become the fireplace hearth; the whole opens to the south with no view of the waterfall at all – only the sound of the roaring water. Wright told Kaufmann, 'I want you to live with the waterfall, not just look at it, but for it to become an integral part of your lives.' Wright noted of Kaufmann, 'he loved the site where the house was built and likes to listen to the waterfall. So that became the prime motive of the design . . . he lives intimately with the thing he loves.'[25] In this Wright is remarkably close to John Dewey, who in his *Art As Experience* (1934), wrote that 'the eye is the sense of distance', while 'sound itself is near, intimate'. Dewey's definition of architecture perfectly describes Fallingwater's massive stone walls and projecting concrete terraces, and the manner in which they make place for haptic experience of bodily position and movement in space: 'Through going out into the environment, position unfolds into volume; through the pressure of the environment, mass is retracted into energy of position, and space remains, when matter is contracted, as an opportunity for further action.'[26]

While in his design of Fallingwater Wright was clearly responding to the provocations of the International Style (including Neutra's Lovell 'Health House' in Los Angeles of 1929, which was visited by 10,000 people when it opened), he again evolved the design from his own earlier works, particularly the cantilevered balconies of the Gale House of 1909 (to the perspective drawing of which he had John Howe add a Fallingwater-like roof trellis in 1935), the stone walls of Taliesin of 1911, the butt-glazed corners of the Freeman House of 1923, and the cantilevered balconies of the Elizabeth Noble Apartments project for Los Angeles of 1929. Yet with the design and construction of Fallingwater, completed in 1937, Wright at age 70 leapt to an astonishing new level, realizing an ideal relation between landscape, architecture and human inhabitation.

In 1936 Wright received the commission to design new corporate offices for the S. C. Johnson and Son Company, manufacturers of floor wax and other household products. Under its president, Herbert F. 'Hib' Johnson, the company had gained a reputation for enlightened management and the provision of a humane work environment, making them a good match for Wright, whose Larkin Building of 30 years earlier was still considered the nation's most progressive office building. Meeting at Taliesin, Johnson and Wright agreed on nothing except their taste in automobiles, for they both owned new streamlined Lincoln Zephyrs, yet in the end

Johnson hired Wright. Wright initially pressed Johnson to relocate the company's offices and factories from Racine, Wisconsin, to an outlying rural area, so as to better exemplify Wright's Broadacre City concept. Stubbornly insisting on this as part of his design, Wright came close to losing the commission, only finally being dissuaded by his wife Oglivanna, who told him: 'Give them what they want, Frank, or you will lose the job.'[27]

The Johnson Wax Company Building, evolved from Wright's unrealized design of 1931 for the *Capital Journal* Building in Salem, Oregon, is composed of a single large, double-height 'great workroom', with columns set in a 6.1-metre (20-ft) square grid, surrounded by a mezzanine with a solid brick wall at the outer edge. The brick outer walls are separated from the mezzanine floor and workroom roof by glazed 'cornices', continuous bands of horizontally stacked Pyrex glass tubing – fabricated for laboratory test tubes – creating an entirely woven sense of light within. The columns, the most extraordinary feature of the building, begin at a 23-centimetre (9-in) diameter base set in a steel cup-shaped footing at the floor, and taper as they rise to the roof, where they open out into 5.48-metre (18-ft) diameter discs or 'petals', each joined to the four adjacent columns by small beams at the tangent points of the discs. The roof between the 'petals' of the columns was glazed with the glass tubing, so that the columns and their umbrella-like 'petals' stand surrounded by light.

Wright based these extraordinary hollow – less than 76 mm (3 in) thick – shell-like concrete structural elements on his studies of the hollow staghorn cholla cactus of Arizona, and his drawings of these 'thin-shell' concrete structures, far *avant la lettre*, required only slight adjustments by Peters and Glickman, an indication of Wright's accurate intuitive grasp of structural principles. In 1937, however, the Wisconsin Building Commission was having none of it, rejecting Wright's column design as incapable of being calculated and in violation of the building code. Wright proposed that a single

Wright (right) at a structural test of a column proposed for the Johnson Wax Building, 4 June 1937. Ben Wiltscheck, the contractor, is on the far left and the client, Hib Johnson, stands to Wright's left.

column be cast and test loaded, and the events of 4 June 1937 would prove the most convincing confirmation of Wright's structural genius.

Surrounded by the owner, contractor, dozens of apprentices and newspaper reporters, including his house client Herbert Jacobs, Wright was at centre stage, directing the loading of sandbags onto the column's petal-like top. The design load was six tons, and at twelve tons the state building inspectors were satisfied – but Wright was not finished yet. 'Keep piling', Jacobs recorded Wright saying, directing that more weight be added until, at 30 tons, Wright walked over and stood directly beneath the column, kicking it and striking it with his cane. By late afternoon no more material could be fitted on the column top; at 60 tons (ten times the design load and five times the doubled safety factor) Wright ordered a crane to pull the braces from the sides and the column fell, smashing a drainpipe buried more than three metres underground.

The serenely top-lit 'great workroom' of the Johnson Wax Building is perhaps Wright's most extraordinary space, a sacred space for work, seeming a world entirely apart from the everyday, and it proved to be a most popular place to work. In later years the company not only reported markedly increased productivity and an unparalleled retention rate among its employees who worked in the space, but was able to recruit the most creative people in the field. As Wright wrote, the Johnson Wax Building was 'designed to be as inspiring to live and work in as any cathedral ever was to worship in.'[28]

Wright was now receiving a steadily increasing stream of commissions, including 'Wingspread', a large house for Hib Johnson, a house for Stanley Marcus, president of the Neiman-Marcus Department Store in Dallas, Texas, and the first of what Wright would call the 'Usonian' Houses, the Robert Lusk House, the C. H. Hoult House, the Paul and Jean Hanna House in Palo Alto, California, and the Herbert Jacobs House in Madison.

The Johnson Wax Building, interior of the 'great workroom'.

In December 1936 Wright became severely ill with pneumonia, and the Fellowship again spent the winter in Chandler, Arizona. It was now apparent that Wright could no longer stand the winters in Wisconsin, and in 1937 he and Oglivanna purchased 800 acres of land on the Maricopa Mesa at the foot of the McDowell Mountains, north of Phoenix, Arizona, for $3.50 per acre. This price was possible because the land had no history of water being found, but this did not discourage Wright, who felt drawn to this beautiful place, and after considerable expense a working well was established. Over the next several years, the entire Fellowship made the week-long trek across the country from Wisconsin to Arizona to spend the five summer months building what Wright would call Taliesin West.

During these trips, the 25 apprentices and Wright's family would often stay at the house of Wright's cousin Richard Lloyd Jones in Tulsa, Oklahoma. It was during one of these stays that Mrs Lloyd Jones recalled for Wright her response to her husband's raging about the fact that the house leaked in numerous places during the frequent Oklahoma downpours: 'Well, this is what you get for leaving a work of art out in the rain.'[29] Wright thought this a superb wisecrack, and would avail himself of it in the future.

In 1937 Wright and the philosopher Baker Brownell collaborated on *Architecture and Modern Life*, a further articulation of Wright's conception of an architecture that would foster American democracy. That same year he was invited to address the All-Union Congress of Architects in Moscow, and he and Oglivanna, who had not been back to Russia since leaving in 1917, made the trip by boat in June. In 1933 Wright had been twice interviewed by *Pravda*, the Communist Party newspaper, saying that at that time, in the midst of the Great Depression, capitalism seemed to be on its last legs. His 1937 speech and interviews he gave while in Russia indicate that he badly misjudged Joseph Stalin's intentions, saying Trotsky was mistaken in claiming Stalin had betrayed the revolution. Based upon his sincere affection for the Russians he met, Wright also characterized the Soviet Union as a fundamentally democratic country. While condemning communism, Wright suggested that capitalism, in principle a good idea, had never really been allowed to blossom due to such corruptions as real estate speculation. Back home, Wright would pay for these comments by being branded as anti-American, a communist sympathizer, and the decade of the 1930s characterized as 'Wright versus America'.[30]

That same year, however, change was in the wind at the Museum of Modern Art. The summer that the Wrights were in Russia, Hitchcock received a letter from the directors of the MoMA to the effect that they were no longer supporting European International Style architecture, and wished to promote American Modernism.[31] John McAndrew, appointed curator of architecture for MoMA in autumn 1937, was made aware of Fallingwater – most likely by Kaufmann himself – and visited the house. The young Finnish architect Alvar Aalto had just been forced to postpone an exhibit, and McAndrew proposed that it be replaced with an exhibit on Fallingwater. This opened in January 1938 and subsequently travelled to ten other cities. Wright's work was also exhibited in Paris that same year, in an exhibit organized by the MoMA titled *Three Centuries of American Art*, the architecture section selected by McAndrew and his assistant, former Taliesin apprentice Elizabeth Bauer Mock (she had recently married fellow Taliesin apprentice Rudolph Mock). McAndrew next proposed a major retrospective on Wright for MoMA, which would take place in 1940.[32]

The year 1938 also marked a high-point of publicity for Wright in other venues, most notably the magazines owned by Henry Luce, founder of *Time* (one million subscribers), *Life* (three million subscribers) and *Fortune*, and who had purchased *Architectural Forum* in 1932. Wright appeared on the cover of *Time* magazine in its 17 January 1938 issue, standing in front of his colour rendering of Fallingwater. The entire issue of the January 1938 *Architectural Forum* was devoted to Wright's work, with a large section on Fallingwater and construction photographs of the Johnson Wax Building, Wingspread, the Hanna House and the Jacobs House. Finally, that same year Wright's design for a prototypical middle-class house, later built for the Schwartz family, was published in *Life* magazine. In June Wright was given an honorary degree by Wesleyan College, where Hitchcock was teaching, and they had a rapprochement that would eventually lead, four years later, to Hitchcock's writing the first definitive monograph on Wright's work.

In the five-year period from 1935 to 1939 Wright received 70 commissions (37 in 1939 alone), and realized 33 buildings. In 1938 Dr Ludd Spivey, president of Florida Southern College, commissioned Wright to design what would eventually constitute the largest collection of Wright buildings in the world in Lakeland, Florida. Among the many house commissions, of particular note are the 'Suntop' Houses in Ardmore, Pennsylvania of 1938, each unit of which consisted of four houses built into a single, outward-opening cluster, an evolution of his early 'Quadruple Block' concept. Finally, in 1939, Wright was invited to deliver the prestigious Sir George Watson lectures for the Sulgrave Manor Board and the Royal Institute of British Architects. Opening the final three of his four lectures with movies taken of life at Taliesin, as well as Taliesin West and other buildings under construction, Wright spoke to the largest audiences ever to attend such an event in London, more than a thousand, composed largely of students and young architects.

That same year Wright had an experience that may well have proved even more satisfying, when he visited the Finnish Pavilion, designed by Alvar Aalto, at the 1939 World's Fair in New York City. Aalto had first received worldwide recognition with his International Style Paimio Sanatorium (1933), but he had recently been evolving a more humane, more natural architecture, reacting strongly against the concept of the 'minimum existence' house put forward by his colleagues in the Congrès Internationaux d'Architecture Moderne (CIAM). Aalto had carefully studied the published images of Wright's Fallingwater, and the impact on the younger architect was immediate, deeply affecting Aalto's design for what many would regard as his greatest work, the Villa Mairea in Noormarkku, completed in 1939. After touring the Finnish Pavilion, the primary feature of which was a two-storey, wave-like wall built entirely of wood, Wright announced that Aalto was 'a genius'.

8

Natural House and the Fountainhead 1939–49

Wright's Usonian or 'Natural' Houses, small houses designed for the American middle class, were what Wright called his greatest achievement as an architect, this because he believed that the house was the fundamental basis of American democracy. Yet Wright also believed the profession had consistently ignored this need: 'The house of moderate cost is not only America's major architectural problem but the problem most difficult for her major architects.'[1] Wright himself has most often been portrayed as an architect for the rich, and by 1939 this had become such a common misrepresentation that Wright himself could employ it against his critics in his lectures in London:

> The modest-cost-house movement is now the thing we are engaged upon for most of our time . . . having built [the Herbert Jacobs House] some of my colleagues, I am told, said that this was a stunt and that I would never build another. But, being of the opinion that to build these houses is the most important thing in our country for an architect to do, I pledged myself to do forty of them. We are now on our twenty-seventh, and I want to assure you that there is nothing more interesting or more important in this world today than trying to put into the houses in which our typical best citizens live something of the quality of a genuine work of art.[2]

The Herbert Jacobs House, Madison, Wisconsin, 1937, interior of living room.

Beginning with the Herbert Jacobs House, built for $5,500 in 1937 for a newspaper reporter and his family in Madison, Wisconsin, Wright developed the Usonian House to be modest in size, from 93 to 140 square metres (1,000 to 1,500 square feet); modest in price, with per-square-foot costs consistently below contemporary market-rate housing; exceedingly energy efficient, using but a small fraction of the energy required by a similar-sized house then and today; orientated to the sun to give the inhabitants daylight throughout the day and year, with solar warming in the winter, and cooling shade and through-ventilation in the summer; employing radiant heating hot water pipes cast into the concrete floor slab; and constructed with modular, standardized, stock components, by non-specialized labour, the building process often supervised by apprentices sent from the Fellowship to live and work on the construction site.

Wright called these houses 'natural' because they were designed to be the background or framework for family life taking place in harmony with nature. Acknowledging the previous history of the sites as agricultural fields, and making experiential the close relationship between agriculture and architecture as related activities of cultivating and transforming the landscape, Wright designed the Usonian House to be integrated with its garden. Typically developed as an L-shape in plan, the house interlocked with its garden, and Wright invariably orientated the garden, and the rooms of the house that opened to it, towards the south. Wright's paired perspective views of the Jacobs House could not be more explicit: the street view is seen from an elevated viewpoint, off the ground, and shows the solid, closed elevation, with horizontal board and batten walls, the only apertures being small clerestory windows set high above the wall and under the roof overhang – the whole an object in the landscape; whereas the garden view is seen from eye-level, on the ground, standing within the garden, enclosed by the wings of the house, with walls of large vertical glass doors opening to the interior – the garden experienced as the most important room of the house. Flooded with sunlight throughout the day and the seasons, the garden court becomes the centre of the Usonian House and the life that went on within it, 'marrying' the house to the earth.

Among the more notable Usonian Houses of this period were the Stanley and Mildred Rosenbaum House (1939), built in Florence, Alabama, for the owners of the local cinema; the house built for the Schwartz family in Two Rivers, Wisconsin, in 1939, based upon Wright's *Life* magazine 'House for a Family of $5,000 a Year Income'; the Loren Pope House (1939) built in Falls Church, Virginia, and designed for a journalist who later wrote a nationally circulated essay titled 'The Love Affair of a Man and His House'; the house designed for *Chicago Daily News* sports editor Lloyd Lewis, Wright's friend since 1918, and his wife Kathryn, built in Libertyville, Illinois, on the Des Plaines River in 1939; the house outside Phoenix for the sisters Rose and Gertrude Pauson of 1939, which had hardly been completed before it was burned to the ground by seasonal renters, its stone walls standing for years as ruins; the house built in Okemos, Michigan, in 1939 for the painters and college professors Alma Goetsch and Katherine Winckler; and the dramatically sited houses built for John Pew in Madison (1938), George Sturges House in Brentwood Heights, Los Angeles (1939), and Gregor Affleck in Bloomfield Hills, Michigan (1940).

Typical of the feelings of all these homeowners about their houses is the comment made in the late 1960s by Samuel Freeman regarding the living room of his concrete block house: 'It has broken planes , different heights . . . the whole thing is like music. I've sat in this room and used it since 1923, and I'm never bored with the room . . . As long as I've lived in this house, this room was always exciting to me. It's almost alive, it's in motion.' This was echoed in a late 1960s interview by Robert Berger, for whom Wright in 1950 designed a house in San Anselmo, California, which Berger built largely by himself: 'It's such a thrill to be feeling a work of art; actually living it. It's almost like a living thing. I'm just overjoyed with the place. My wife, of course, is mad at me because I never really want to go anywhere – I just want to stay home.' Wright's apprentice John Howe recalls that Wright 'had tremendous rapport with all his clients. Even though they would come for just a $5,000 house, he made each client feel as if it were the most important thing to him. Mr. Wright would closet himself with them in his office because he liked to work with them in person.'[3]

Wright has been so consistently characterized as behaving egotistically and having a high-handed attitude towards his clients that comments such as that of Sarah Smith, client with her husband Melvyn for a Usonian House in Bloomfield Hills, Michigan, in 1946, come as somewhat of a shock:

> Frank Lloyd Wright was just the most humble person. His humility was so great, so different from what one heard about in the press . . . you used to hear about his arrogance and about his not being able to get along with the press. But really knowing that man – he was so beautiful, so wonderful, so easy to talk to. I enjoyed every minute that I was with him.

Wright's apprentice Aaron Green recalls Wright often saying that 'the newspaper didn't print the twinkle in his eye . . . And, with very few exceptions, it was always there – that twinkle – when he made the kind of statement that would later be offered as evidence of his irascibility.' Buckminster Fuller noted,

> In public, he had a histrionic sense. When he got on the stage he really enjoyed tremendously playing a part, and he enjoyed tremendously shocking people . . . But when you were alone with Frank Lloyd Wright, in his own chambers, he became not only modest but really a very humble child. He was a very beautiful human being as I knew him.'[4]

Life at Taliesin was determined largely by Wright's personality and daily schedule, and his memories of his own 'education' on the Lloyd Jones farm and in the office of Adler and Sullivan. The apprentices' day started well before dawn for those with kitchen duty, and at 6.00 am for the others. Breakfast was followed by a half-hour of choral practice of works by Bach, Palestrina and César Franck, under the guidance of Svetlana Wright Peters. By 8.00 am half the apprentices were in the drafting room, the other half were out on the farm or the construction sites. There was a break at

A Taliesin Sunday gathering; Wright sits on the dais.

noon for lunch and a brief rest in their rooms, and then on again until 5.00 pm. Dinner was at 6.00 pm, and evenings were free. On Saturday nights the apprentices, as well as neighbours from surrounding communities and guests, were invited to a movie in the theatre at Hillside. On Sunday mornings ecumenical services were held at the Lloyd Jones Chapel, and in the afternoons Wright would lead the assembled group, along with invited guests, into the hills for a picnic, gala events for which everyone dressed in appropriate attire. Sunday evenings were reserved for concerts by the apprentices, each of whom was expected to develop a musical talent, as well as Wright's celebrated talks, all of which took place in the Taliesin living room.

Wright's own schedule, described by the apprentices as typically a fifteen-hour day, usually began at 4.00 am, when he would rise and work at the drafting board in his own bedroom, or come and wake his chief apprentice Howe so they could work together in the studio. One morning Carter Manny, later the director of the Graham Foundation, remembers that, just as breakfast was concluding, Wright emerged from his bedroom, a sheaf of drawings in his hand, and led the way to the studio, where he spread out the drawings, documenting the designs for three different houses.

> On each sheet plan, section and elevation were superimposed on top of one another forming wondrous abstractions, but actually concisely depicting multiple aspects of each conception. After a brief explanation, each drawing was turned over to a senior apprentice . . . I was astounded by this experience. Imagine, three designs in roughly three and a half hours. This was a virtuoso performance[5]

– yet a typical one for Wright.

Wright attended to his extensive correspondence with clients, friends, fellow architects and assorted social, business and cultural leaders in the morning, after lunch, and in the evenings. Wright came back into the studio in the mid-morning, and again in the mid-afternoon, moving from one apprentice's board to the next, correcting and developing the numerous designs. Howe recalled that 'Wright had great patience at the drafting board . . . he would work tirelessly, often spending hours on certain presentation drawings . . . Invariably a group would gather around when Mr Wright was working at the drafting board. Mr Wright enjoyed an audience. He was a teacher, although he said he wasn't.'[6] In the evenings Wright went to bed soon after supper, and the lights at Taliesin were turned out at 8.00 pm in the early years, 10.00 pm in later years.

Despite being in his seventies, working with his much younger apprentices seemed to rejuvenate Wright, both physically and intellectually. Marcus Weston recalled the time he was replacing the board and batten siding on the 'Romeo and Juliet' windmill of 1896. He saw Wright below on the ground at the base of the tower, and the next moment, having ascended the ladder, he suddenly appeared at the top – a difficult climb for the much younger

Weston.[7] Yen Liang, who came from China and studied at Yale, Massachusetts Institute of Technology and Cornell before joining the Fellowship, recalled playing a Vivaldi violin sonata, accompanied by Edgar Tafel on piano, at one of the Sunday musicals in the Taliesin living room. Afterwards Wright asked about the composer and, discovering that Antonio Vivaldi was a predecessor of Johann Sebastian Bach, said, 'So, Bach did have someone before him to base his work on.' In the drafting room, Liang remembered Wright's wry remark, which should be interpreted as regarding his own reputed infallibility: 'The eraser is the most important instrument of the architectural design.'[8]

In 1939 Wright hired the young photographer Pedro Guerrero to document the Taliesin Fellowship, a relationship that would last the rest of Wright's life and result in some of the most remarkable portraits of Wright. Wright himself was a superb photographer, able to estimate exactly the time the camera shutter should stay open under widely differing light conditions. Always sensitive about his height, Wright choreographed many of Guerrero's photographs to ensure he was shown from a flattering vantage point. Wright shortened the legs of all chairs at his desk save his own, in order that he might appear equal in height to those sitting across from him, as well as scaling the ceilings and doors to his own modest dimension, 'as the tall ones soon learned painfully in Taliesin with banged heads, with no consolation from [Wright's] Olympian advice that anyone over five feet ten [a height Wright did not attain even when wearing lifts in his shoes] was "a weed", grown beyond nature's norm.' Wright enjoyed needling his son-in-law Wes Peters about his height – 1.93 metres (6 ft 4 in) – saying, 'Sit down, Wes, you're spoiling the scale of the room.'[9]

By 1939 Taliesin West was largely complete, and starting that year the Fellowship spent the five winter months of each year in the Arizona desert. Constructed largely by the apprentices, the thick battered walls of Taliesin West were built of large desert boulders

Taliesin West, Scottsdale, Arizona, 1937–9, apprentices putting canvas on roof frames.

set in concrete formwork so as to be exposed and appear as if they have been excavated from the site. Spanning between the walls were angled wood beams, which in turn held the stretched canvas-clad wood frames of the roof. The stone walls appeared to grow out of the desert floor, while the wood and canvas roofs were placed upon them like the lid of a pot. All the spaces opened directly to the desert, and the canvas was rolled, hinged and tied, using sail rigging cords, to allow the breezes to be directed through the space at different times of the day. Taliesin West fuses the permanent, in the stone walls and the large boulder with Native American markings at the entry, indicating prior occupation of the site, and the

Taliesin West exterior, recent photograph.

Wright and Edgar Kaufmann sitting in Taliesin West living room, *c.* 1948.

ephemeral and seasonal, in the annual replacement of the canvas roofs and window flaps. Taliesin West, one of Wright's greatest works, achieves a perfect integration of its landscape, climate, local materials and the experience of inhabiting the desert.

The buildings at Florida Southern College would continue construction throughout this decade, starting with the Anne Pfeiffer Chapel (1939), the Seminar Building (1940), the Library (1941), the Industrial Arts Building (1942) and the Administration Building (1945). Responding to the campus site in an existing lakeside citrus grove, Wright designed each structure to be divided horizontally at its middle, at the line of the tree canopy, below being custom-cast concrete blocks, fabricated by student labour, with coloured glass squares inset, which served as the base or ground floor of the buildings, and above being concrete block and cast-concrete walls finished with smooth stucco. Thus when walking along the connecting arcades, in the shadows of the citrus tree canopy, one experienced up close the delicately patterned tan-coloured concrete block walls, while from a distance one would see the white, smooth walls rising above the trees. The Pfeiffer Chapel itself restates the larger theme of the campus, as from the shadow of the tree canopy one enters a low, dimly lit space at the periphery, with square spots of coloured light entering through the concrete block, from which one moves out into the tall, brightly lit central space of the sanctuary, with its glazed tower, connecting the interior directly to the sky.

In 1940 Wright created the Frank Lloyd Wright Foundation, which would henceforth own the Fellowship buildings and its works as a tax-exempt foundation. That same year the New York publisher Duell, Sloan and Pearce agreed to publish three books by Wright, beginning with Frederick Gutheim's *Frank Lloyd Wright on Architecture*, a collection of Wright's writings. This would later be followed by a monograph by Hitchcock and a revised and updated version of *An Autobiography*. Also that year Wright received the

Gold Medal from the RIBA, Britain's highest architectural honour.

But the most important event of 1940, and one that Wright had been working towards for several years, was the exhibition of his work at New York's Museum of Modern Art, which opened in November. In 1939 John McAndrew, the curator for the MoMA, had visited Taliesin to determine with Wright what was to be shown in the exhibit. Since then Wright's apprentices had been working feverishly to build twenty large models. There was also to be a catalogue, organized by Hitchcock, with essays by Walter Behrendt (Mumford's German friend), Talbot Hamlin, Fiske Kimball, Grant Carpenter Manson, Richard Neutra, Alvar Aalto, Harwell Hamilton Harris, Mies van der Rohe, Edgar, Liliane and Junior Kaufmann, McAndrew and Hitchcock. In reviewing the essays, however, Wright was outraged by Behrendt's statement implying that Wright's work did not embrace contemporary living conditions: Wright objected that, if such were in fact the case, then no one should hire Wright as their architect. With Wright threatening to cancel the exhibit, McAndrew had no choice but to open the exhibit without the accompanying catalogue, and the essays remained unpublished for 65 years.

For Wright, the critical part of the exhibit was the construction of a full-size Usonian House in the garden of the MoMA, which could not only be visited by the exhibit attendees, but also be viewed from the gallery floors above, where the exhibit would be on display. The critical part of the MoMA garden needed to build the house, however, was not owned by the museum but by John D. Rockefeller Jr, whose brother Nelson was on the museum's board of directors. Ignoring the actual cost data Wright had assembled from other Usonians, Rockefeller did not believe Wright's Usonian was an answer to America's low-cost housing problem, stating that 'it does not seem to me that the proposed building is economical either to build, to maintain or to operate.' The chairman of the museum's board agreed with Rockefeller, saying of Wright's

Usonian House: 'as an answer to solve the cheap housing problem, it is ridiculous.'[10] Wright's Exhibition Usonian House was not built, and the exhibit opened without it.

During the years preceding the Second World War Wright increasingly believed that, compared to his own work, International Style architecture was fundamentally heartless. When asked his opinion of modern architecture in Europe, Wright replied, 'What modern architecture needs today, young man, is more love.' This may account for his often rude reception of many European modernists who endeavoured to visit Taliesin. When Walter Gropius came to the University of Wisconsin in nearby Madison to lecture in 1937, the faculty called Taliesin to say Gropius wished to visit. Wright's reply was brusque, saying he had no desire to meet 'Herr Gropius. What he stands for and what I stand for are poles apart. Our ideas will never merge. In a sense, we're professional enemies – but he's an outside enemy. At least I'm staying in my own country.' Yet this also reflected Wright's resentment of his own situation at home. In 1940 Gropius invited Wright to Harvard to give a lecture, and they had two hours of undisturbed talk at the Gropius house in Lincoln, Massachusetts. Gropius recalled that Wright 'complained bitterly about the treatment he had received in his own country. He referred particularly to the fact that I had been made Chairman of the Department of Architecture at Harvard, whereas he himself had never been offered such a position of influence when he was younger.'[11]

Wright's opposition to US intervention in the European war grew steadily stronger, and he wrote ten increasingly strident essays from 1940 to 1942, including the remarkably prescient 'Of What Use is a Great Navy with No Place to Hide?' of 1941, which predicted the events of that December at Pearl Harbor. Fuelling Wright's virulent anti-war rhetoric were his long-standing pacifism, his fond memories of Germany, Japan and Italy as countries that welcomed him and his architecture, and his growing fear that war would again destroy his practice, which was at that moment only just recovering from the Great Depression. Wright consistently argued that America's only real salvation and defence lay in building a truly democratic society, 'in ordered decentralization, in social reintegration with the ground, in a natural capitalist economy.'[12]

In this same 1941 essay on the naval build-up, Wright stated that America should not imitate Germany's warmongering, but rather develop its own inner strengths: 'No, our real enemy is not Hitler! Our real enemy lies in our own timidity and stupidity as seen in this frightful current so smoothly moved, coaxed in the direction of self-destruction.'[13] This brought an immediate response from the vehemently interventionist Mumford, who wrote to Wright: 'you use the word gangster, not to characterize Hitler and his followers, but to castigate those who would fight to the death rather than see Hitler's "new order" prevail in any part of the earth . . . You dishonor the generous impulses you once ennobled. Be silent!' Wright wrote back to Mumford: 'There is no good Empire: there never was a just war . . . Organic character is the basis of true greatness in [any culture] or in any individual or in any nation. War is the negation of all these potentialities now as ever and forever.'[14] Wright and Mumford would not speak or write to one another again for ten years.

In his anti-war essays, Wright argued for American democracy as a model, not as the world's policeman: 'Believing in democracy, however, I fail to see what right we have as a nation to say to this or that other nation, "You are all wet. Get democratic or we'll blow you out of the water."' Wright believed that entering the war would cause America to move away from democracy, based upon the dignity of the individual, and towards what he called 'mobocracy', based upon the mediocrity of the mob: 'Dictatorship is inevitable to mobocracy. We already have it in conscription in peacetime.' Conscription was a particularly perilous threat to Taliesin, and Wright fought it in deed and letter: 'As for conscription, I think it has deprived every young man in America of the honor and privilege of dedicating himself as a freeman to the service of his country. They are all condemned without a hearing and enslaved. Were I born forty years later . . . I too should be a conscientious objector.'[15]

Nineteen of Wright's Taliesin apprentices were drafted and entered the armed forces, Howe, Weston and Davy Davison were sentenced to prison for refusing to be drafted, and Curtis Besinger and Howard Tenbrink were sent to conscientious objector camps. By 1943 only Wright's son-in-law Peters, his secretary Masselink and Caraway remained at Taliesin. Wright's encouraging resistance to the draft among his apprentices, together with his inflammatory anti-war rhetoric in his published essays, had also brought him to the attention of the FBI, where the director J. Edgar Hoover began a file of memos regarding Wright's purportedly anti-American activities. Following the banner year of 1939, with 37 commissions and 15 built, in the six years from 1940 to 1945 Wright received a total of 80 commissions, of which only 18 were built.

Wright was forced to abandon Taliesin West temporarily during this period, and he settled in for the long winters in Wisconsin. Hitchcock had for several years been visiting Taliesin to research the monograph Wright had hired him to write. Before the war, apprentices Tafel and Mosher had been assigned to help Wright and Hitchcock sort through the drawings in the disorganized archives, and Wright had a number of new drawings made when the originals were not suitable for reproduction. Wright, intrigued at the sight of drawings of old designs he had forgotten, scandalized the scholarly Hitchcock by both back-dating drawings, to make the designs look even more avant-garde than they already were, and taking a pencil and making changes to archive drawings, redesigning and perfecting them. For Wright architecture and design were never finished, and he consistently refused to consider his older drawings either sacred or not subject to further refinement.

Wright was equally as insistent on designing the layout for the book itself. His format required square pages, with a planning grid created by a second, smaller square placed over the primary square in an asymmetrical position. Illustrations and all text blocks, including captions, were to be fitted into this pattern, which could be varied almost infinitely, yet always resulted in a harmony of proportions. Hitchcock recalled the often humorous result: 'the size of the caption was determined not only by what you had put in it, but by what space you needed to fill out the pattern. So, some captions would be no more than four words and other captions might go up to a quarter of a page.'[16]

The result of Hitchcock's labours was *In the Nature of Materials: The Buildings of Frank Lloyd Wright 1887–1941* (1942), which for more than 50 years remained the only comprehensive monograph on Wright's work. The next year Wright completed his triple contract with publisher Duell, Sloan and Pearce by issuing a revised and updated version of his bestselling *An Autobiography*. The publication of *Space, Time and Architecture* (1941) by Sigfried Giedion, the Swiss historian and founder of CIAM who had been brought to Harvard in 1938 by Gropius, effectively canonized the Modern Movement. Giedion placed Wright and Sullivan in a section titled 'American Development', which preceded the main section titled 'Space-Time in Art, Architecture, and Construction', thus once again marginalizing Wright as a precursor to true Modernism.

During the Second World War only a few projects came into Wright's office, but among them were several that would prove crucial to the final phase of Wright's career. In 1943, at the age of 76, Wright was commissioned to design a museum to house the Solomon R. Guggenheim Collection of Non-Objective Painting, one of the most comprehensive collections of modern abstract paintings in the world, including works by Wassili Kandinsky, Piet Mondrian, Ferdinand Leger, László Moholy-Nagy, Robert Delaunay, Rudolf Bauer and Albert Gleizes. Wright was chosen by the curator of the collection, Baroness Hilla Rebay von Ehrenweisen, who had read all three books on Wright published by Duell, Sloan and Pearce, and who asked that he design a 'Temple of Non-Objectivity'. After receiving the commission, Wright toured New York City in the summer of 1944 with his cousin, Robert Moses, the City's Parks Commissioner, looking at possible sites for the museum. While Wright favoured a site in the park Moses had recently opened north of the city, Rebay and Guggenheim had determined that the museum would be on a downtown New York site.

Wright's first schemes for the Guggenheim were based upon his 1926 Automobile Objective, an unbuilt project designed for Gordon Strong on a site on Sugarloaf Mountain, Maryland, where he had proposed a continuously inward spiralling concrete automobile ramp enclosing a planetarium at the centre. For the Guggenheim Museum, from the start Wright conceived of an open central top-lit space surrounded by a pedestrian ramp that would serve as a continuous gallery. Wright experimented with circular spirals that grew smaller as they rose, as well as with hexagonal and square ramps, finally settling in 1945 on a circular spiral that grew larger, opening as it rose. In 1949, after years of delay, due primarily to post-war construction cost inflation, Solomon Guggenheim died and his nephew Harry Guggenheim took over the project. It was not until 1951, however, that the museum's Fifth Avenue site, facing Central Park, was finally purchased, and it would be thirteen long years after Wright was commissioned before construction started on the museum.

In 1944 Wright was commissioned by the Herbert Jacobs family to build a second house, located on the family farm. The extraordinary design, called by Wright the 'Solar Hemicycle', distilled the energy-efficient siting concepts of the Usonians into an almost perfect construction. The two-storey plan is curved to create a semicircle, its inner side opened to the warm south sun by continuous full-height glazing, and its outer edge closed to the cold north winds by solid rock walls and an earth berm. The mounded hill cradling the carved garden created a powerful sense of place on the flat prairie.

That same year Wright designed and built the Research Tower of the Johnson Wax Building in Racine, his first realization of his tree-concept of cantilevering the floor structure from a central massive core column, initially proposed in the 1923 National Insurance Company Building and later perfected in the St Marks-in-the-Bouwerie project of 1929. In the Johnson Wax Tower, circular mezzanine office floors alternated with square laboratory floors, and the building's outer skin of bands of brick and horizontal glass tubing provided light but no views, making the tower – a building type normally extrovert in character – as introverted as the original office building of 1936.

In 1938, after arranging to meet Wright in New York, the Russian writer Ayn Rand had sent Wright the first three chapters of *The Fountainhead*, her novel about architects. Wright had given them to Tafel to read, who apparently passed them on to a younger apprentice, and the review that came back to Rand from Wright was decidedly discouraging. Undaunted if disappointed, Rand, who had researched the book by working in the office of the Art Deco architect Ely Jacques Kahn, published the novel in 1943 and her philosophy of selfishness, capitalism and the individual over the collective created a furor.

Wright is patently the model for Rand's architect hero, Howard Roark, and the parallels to Wright's life, as told in *An Autobiography*, are many: the older mentor (Sullivan); the offer of fame in a successful classical practice (Burnham); the years in exile working in the country (Taliesin); the extramarital affair outside the law (Cheney); the evil critic who supports the classical style (Kimball?); the super-capitalist, self-made clients (Kaufmann and Johnson); and the dramatic house on a cliff (Fallingwater). Yet Rand also misrepresented key aspects of Wright's philosophy of democracy. Despite Roark voicing such 'Wrightian' ideals as 'unborrowed vision', America being based upon individualism, and the need for integrity in both buildings and men, Wright also held that in a true democracy 'neither land nor money nor creative ideas can be speculative commodities to be traded or held over by someone against the common good'. This was a decidedly unselfish concept that, despite Wright calling it 'natural capitalism', would be almost impossible to classify as 'capitalist' in any of that concept's usually understood meanings.[17]

By 1944, in anticipation of post-war reconstruction, the issue of monumentality, and the fact that the Modern Movement was predicated to a large degree on anti-monumental conceptions of architecture's place and function in society, had emerged as a common concern among leading architects, critics and historians. A debate on the issue ensued between Sigfried Giedion, who had recently canonized the International Style, and Lewis Mumford, who championed the American modern architecture of Richardson, Sullivan and Wright. By the mid-1940s a rare unanimity had emerged, holding that an appropriate modern form of collective monumentality was needed, and that the housing-based design formulas of the International Style were incapable of addressing it. In this, Wright was well ahead of the critics, having a full generation earlier engaged in the development of an appropriately American form of monumentality in works such as Unity Temple, the Larkin Building, the Midway Gardens and the Imperial Hotel. During this debate George Howe, then Louis Kahn's partner, and whose work had been shown in the 1932 MoMA International Style exhibit, singled out Wright's Unity Temple as an exemplary modern monument particularly appropriate for American democracy.[18]

Indeed, despite his unceasing anti-war rhetoric, Wright emerged from this fallow period with his public fame if anything increased, due to his three widely read publications, and his reputation among his colleagues equally enhanced. This last was exemplified by the 'summit meeting' luncheon held in honour of Wright and Alvar Aalto at the Manhattan Club in New York on 23 November 1945, and sponsored by such American architectural luminaries as George Howe, Edward Durrell Stone, Philip Johnson and Wallace Harrison, as well as *Architectural Forum* editor Howard Meyers and the urban visionary Hugh Ferris. Aalto was being courted by both Harvard and MIT for a teaching post, but he wrote most excitedly to his wife Aino about Wright's invitation for breakfast, 'three hours of really pleasant conversation' at the Plaza Hotel, and his subsequent visit to Taliesin.

Aalto and Wright rode the 260 kilometres from Milwaukee, where the latter had given a lecture and his work was being exhibited, to Taliesin in one of Wright's Cherokee-red automobiles. Of his stay Aalto wrote:

> Supper just as in the photographs; Frank, Oglivanna and me in the special seats of honor, the boys and girls passing the food around small Japanese tables. Then music and performances by the students, each in turn. Slept like a log for ten hours. Today I have strolled around. The place is agreeable and the atmosphere is right. The school is much bigger than you'd think, though some of the rooms are so low that FLW's son-in-law, an architect of course, can't stand up straight in them. The main drawing office is about 40 × 30 meters, and there are many different [apprentices' rooms surrounding the drafting room], all built by the students and local farm boys with their own hands. I am enclosing a landscape sketch of the view from the window at which I am writing this letter.[19]

During this trip Aalto also was taken by Wes Peters to visit a number of Wright's built works along the Lake Michigan waterfront, including the Johnson Wax Buildings in Racine. Peters recalled that the trip took longer than he anticipated because every time they would get back onto the highway, Aalto, whom Peters said 'was well on his way to becoming an alcoholic', 'would decide it was time to stop for some coffee, which meant he really wanted a drink.' That evening Peters took Aalto to Karl Ratzsch's famous German restaurant in Milwaukee, where he and Wright had eaten many times before the war, but where they had not been in more than five years. Arriving at the restaurant, Peters was dismayed to see 'a huge line of people. I thought what a terrible thing. Here I have this foreign guest, and I had told him how good the restaurant was, and here we couldn't possibly get into it.' At that moment, Mrs Ratzsch spotted Peters and called out, '"Mr Peters, your table is ready now. Is Mr Wright with you?"'[20] Peters's description of Aalto's legendary drinking was in marked contrast to Wright, who neither smoked nor drank alcohol his entire life.

In autumn 1946 tragedy again struck the Wright family when Svetlana, Wright's stepdaughter and Wes Peter's wife, lost control of her car and crashed off a bridge into a river, killing herself and one of her two sons. Oglivanna never really recovered from this blow and was for some time unwilling to ride in automobiles. With the end of the war also came several bitter professional disappointments for Wright. Perhaps the most aggravating of these was when Edgar Kaufmann hired Richard Neutra to design his second great house at Palm Springs, California, in 1945; the spectacular national publicity the house received, starting in 1947, was largely orchestrated by Kaufmann. Wright's dislike of Neutra, who had written a perceptive and laudatory essay on Wright's engagement of technology and materials for the aborted MoMA catalogue of 1940, was compounded when Ayn Rand, for whom Wright designed a house in 1946, chose instead to purchase an existing Neutra-designed house in Palm Springs.

Indeed, to Wright it seemed the International Style architects were everywhere he went in those days. In 1947 Wright attended an international conference at Princeton University, where he found

Gropius also among the presenters, and again in Mexico City, where the national government had invited them both to speak at the opening of the new University. The Mexican-German architect Max Cetto invited Wright and Gropius to an evening discussion with the leading Mexican architects. Wright arrived as Gropius was expounding on his ideal of collaborative teamwork in architecture, exemplified by The Architects' Collaborative, his own practice recently opened in Boston. Wright argued instead for primacy of the individual maker, implying that designing a work of architecture was an act of love: 'But Walter, when you want to make a child you don't ask for the help of your neighbor.' Gropius countered, 'If the neighbor happens to be a woman, I might,' making Wright laugh, and Gropius recalled that 'this was the only time I managed to have the last word in skirmishes with the quick-witted master.'[21] However, the strong influence Wright's work exerted over the designs by Cetto and Luis Barragán for El Pedregal, their new housing development in Mexico City, including Barragán's use of the image of Wright's Fallingwater in a 1951 advertisement for the project, indicate that, if Gropius won the skirmish that day, Wright won the larger battle.

By 1946 there were 65 apprentices at Taliesin and Taliesin West, by far the largest number ever, and in the next three years Wright would receive 125 commissions, with 43 designs being built. It was during this post-war building boom that a schism became noticeable in Wright's work, with his larger and more expensive commissions, usually proposed to be constructed of cast-in-place concrete, progressively losing the integration of space, function, construction, scale and site – the very traits Wright had earlier considered fundamental to his architecture. At the same time, the Usonian Houses, comprising the vast majority of Wright's commissions and built works during the last dozen years of his life, were inevitably limited in terms of budget and stock materials, yet nevertheless exhibited a consistent balance of spatial invention, experiential order and human scale. Before the turn of the century Wright had written that limitations are the architect's best friends, and this truism is nowhere more evident that in the contrast that developed among Wright's own works of this period.

Public works from this period deserving note include the Butterfly Wing Bridge for Spring Green, and the Roger Lacy Hotel for Dallas, Texas, both of 1946 and both unrealized. For the hotel, Wright proposed a twelve-storey base that filled the urban block and formed an atrium court at its centre, out of which rose a forty-storey tower – a concept that would later be employed to design dozens of American hotels starting in the 1970s, without any credit to Wright as the source of its inspiration. The bridge, initially designed to serve as a model for bridges of the national and state highway systems (and three years later evolved into a competition entry to replace the San Francisco Bay Bridge), is a striking example of the plasticity of reinforced concrete, and presaged the contemporary work of the engineer and architect Santiago Calatrava.

While the Unitarian Church built in Shorewood Hills, Wisconsin, in 1947 shows Wright at his best, with its stone walls and beautifully folded roof and glazed 'prow' behind the altar, other increasingly grandiose projects indicate the steady deterioration of Wright's commitment to his own fundamental principles. Particularly revealing are his designs for the Play Resort, Hotel, Sports Club and cottages of 1947 for Huntington Hartford, intended for a site at the edge of the desert in Los Angeles. The Sports Club was to be a collection of flying saucer-shaped concrete discs cantilevered off an enormous triangular rock-clad abutment, with the water of the swimming pool spilling over the rim and falling into the canyon below. This last is a crude display of the wealth of Wright's client in this arid, water-starved region, made all the more remarkable when we remember that the Los Angeles region was at that time still being subjected to the famous 'water wars', which pitted private land developers against the local elected government for control of severely limited water supplies.

On the other hand, it was also during this period that Wright developed what he called his 'Usonian Automatics', indicating that their components were so modular and logical that they could be assembled by unskilled labour, even by the clients themselves – a task a number of them found to be not quite as easy as the name 'automatic' implied. The Usonian Houses from this period reached an unprecedented level of elegance, efficiency and constructive refinement, as well as remarkable variety, from the Alvin Miller House (1946) built in Charles City, Iowa, the Herman Mossberg House (1946) built in South Bend, Indiana, the Melvyn Smith House (1946) built in Bloomfield Hills, Michigan, the various houses designed and built for the development of Usonia in Pleasantville, New York, starting in 1947, to the house built for Mrs Clinton Walker in Carmel, California, in 1949.

In 1948, as the post-war suburban housing building boom was in full swing, *Architectural Forum* for a second time dedicated an entire issue to Wright's work. He believed that his concept for Broadacre City was, if anything, more relevant after the Second World War than it had been before, and he responded with a vengeance when his cousin Robert Moses publicly criticized urban planning proposals such as Broadacre City. In 1944 Moses had published an article in the *New York Times* magazine entitled 'Mr. Moses Dissects the "Long Haired Planners": The Park Commissioner Prefers Common Sense to Their Revolutionary Theories', in which he claimed all urban regionalists were communist, called Mumford 'an outspoken revolutionary', [22] characterized Wright as 'brilliant but erratic', and stated that Wright was 'regarded in Russia as our greatest builder'. Speaking to Wright directly, Moses said it was his staff's feeling that 'you would get further if you tried an experiment on a reasonable scale, frankly called an experiment and refrained from announcing that it was the pattern of all future American living.' Wright titled his reply 'To the Mole', a reference to Moses's tunnelling of highways under New York City rivers, and attacked the idea that more highways connecting the city to the countryside was the answer: 'And to hell with the voracity of our amazing materialism! Speed is a kind of voracity.' Wright went on to say that American young people returning from the war 'have not only the right to find their own initiative released on their own soil. They have an even better right to find their own lives in their own hands, at last', referring again to Wright's arguments against making speculative commodities of land, money and ideas.[23]

Throughout the thirteen years Wright was designing the Guggenheim Museum, from 1943 until construction began in earnest in 1956, Moses publicly and privately criticized Wright's designs, railing against both the collection of abstract paintings, which Moses despised, and the boldly curving building Wright was designing to house them. In 1947 Wright wrote an essay entitled 'Prejudice, Sir, is a Disease', in which he noted that Moses's attitude towards new ideas was exemplary of the reason why 'New York City has earned the reputation of being the most provincial city in these United States.' Wright warned that 'should any power-prophet with any "edifice-complex", his very own or not, ever successfully interfere in [the building of the Guggenheim] New York City would lose its only real claim to charm: freedom of choice in all human variety.' Saying Moses only wanted to see a museum that looked like those he had seen before, Wright wrote: 'A thorough-bred like the splendid gift of the Solomon R. Guggenheim Museum is bound to make the official bristle because it is no pagan idol either of ancient or modern times.'[24] Despite the apparent rancour of this exchange, we shall see that, before the Guggenheim Museum story was finished, Moses would have one more – entirely unexpected – part to play.

As the decade concluded, Wright was once again ascendant, publishing *Genius and the Mobocracy* (1949), his wide-ranging profile of Louis Sullivan and his time, and receiving the Gold Medal from the American Institute of Architects, a group he had never deigned to join. In his AIA acceptance speech Wright was gracious even as he suggested that a prophet is rarely honoured in their own country; 'Honors have reached me from almost every great nation in the world. Honor has, however, been a long time coming from home. But here it is at last. Handsomely, indeed.' Wright went on:

> But I do want to say to you tonight something that may account in some measure for the fact that I have not been a member of your professional body – that I have consistently maintained amateur status . . . Now – of course Architecture – capital A – is in the gutter . . . it is Science that is ruining us in Architecture and Art as it has already ruined Religion, as it has already made a monkey of Philosophy. Already Science has practically destroyed us spiritually and is sending us into perpetual war.

Wright argued that, despite possessing the greatest riches and materials in the world, '*we have built nothing for the Democracy we profess. We have built nothing* in the spirit of the great freedom that has been ours.'

In answer to this charge, Wright argued that architects must seek and work with the nature of all things, stated in terms strikingly similar to those that would be used ten years later by Louis Kahn: 'what could save us but an *innate sense of honor*? . . . what would be the honor of, say, a brick? To be a *brick* brick, wouldn't it? A *good* brick . . . Now – what the honor of the man? To be a true man – *an individual*. To live up to this ideal of individuality we call Democracy.' Arguing against America's newest war, the 'cold war' with communism, Wright then concluded with an argument as valid today as when he made it:

With a good conscience we wouldn't be pursuing a cold war –
we would be pursuing a great endeavor to plant, rear and nurture
a true civilization at no matter what cost. We would then soon
have the kind of culture that would be sure to convince the whole
world that we had the right idea. We'd have all the Russians
coming in here on us, learning from us, willing to work for us or
with us, not afraid that we were going to destroy them or destroy
anybody else.[25]

As if to add insult to injury, at the moment that Wright was
subjecting his AIA peers to this tongue-lashing, he was simultaneously attacking mediocrity, conformity and fashionable architectural form through his representation, only thinly disguised, in
the hit movie *The Fountainhead*, released in 1949. This was directed
by King Vidor, with a screenplay by Ayn Rand, and starred Gary
Cooper as Howard Roark. Wright had apparently declined to
design the sets for the movie, and as a result they tended more
towards Neutra than Wright, yet the parallels between the film's
story and Wright's life could hardly have been more precise. A previously unnoticed aspect of the film is that Gary Cooper's voice and
diction sound remarkably like Wright, suggesting that Rand had
the actor study tapes of Wright lecturing. *The Fountainhead* ends
with Roark standing atop the city's tallest building, under construction to his design. Some have suggested that this proves that
Rand's hero was not modelled on Wright, with his well-known
'scorn for skyscrapers'.[26] Yet in this Rand was not so much histor-
ically accurate as she was prescient, since, in an astonishing case of
life imitating art, the next decade would see Wright propose the
world's tallest skyscraper, the 'Mile High'.

Usonia Lost and Found 1949–59

Wright's last decade was by far his most productive as an architect, social critic and cultural innovator. From 1950, at the age of 83, to the spring of 1959, at the age of almost 92, Wright designed 346 projects – more than one quarter of his entire life's work – with 137 buildings constructed. It is startling to realize that this astonishing number of commissions came at a time when Wright was being declared to be irrelevant by most critics in the US, a relic of a bygone era whose peak was achieved before the Second World War – if not before the First. It was in this same decade that Alvar Aalto inscribed on his boat the ancient Roman saying, *Nemo Propheta in Patria* ('No one is a prophet in their own country'), and this could have served equally well as a motto for Wright during his last ten years. Yet he had learned to fight fire with fire, and his skills at employing the press to his own advantage during the 1950s would prove formidable.

In 1951, the Henry Luce publication *Architectural Forum* dedicated its third complete issue to Wright's work, for the first time containing full-colour photographs illustrating the Johnson Wax Research Tower, the Florida Southern College buildings and five of the Usonian Houses, including the second Herbert Jacobs House, the 'Solar Hemicycle'. In the accompanying essay, pointedly titled 'Whatever His Age . . . To the Young Man in Architecture', Wright wrote: 'The Machine has yet nowhere given to America the flower of indigenous culture. The Machine has so far produced for us only the weeds of a Civilization.' Wright's distinction between a universal civilization, brought by industrialization, and a local culture, source of community and identity, precisely presaged the almost identical arguments of philosophers that would first be heard ten years later.[1]

Wright called his visionary, idealized American democracy 'Usonia', and though no one else has been able to find it there, he maintained his source was in the writings of Samuel Butler:

> author of *The Way of All Flesh*, originator of the modern realistic novel in his *Erewhon* ("nowhere" spelled backwards), pitied us for having no name of our own. "The United States" did not appear to him a good title for us as a nation and the word "American" belonged to us only in common with a dozen or more countries. So he suggested USONIAN – roots of the word in the word unity or in *union*. This seemed to me appropriate.'[2]

For Wright the primary vehicle for realizing Usonia remained the Usonian House, and during his last decade he designed and built hundreds of them, including the Raymond Carlson House (1950) in Phoenix, Arizona. This extremely inexpensive house for the editor of *Arizona Highways* magazine is built of 10 × 10 centimetre (4 × 4 in) redwood posts, exposed inside and out and painted turquoise blue, with grey concrete stucco panels infilling between, and is perhaps the closest Wright ever came to traditional Japanese house construction. Wright was so pleased with the final outcome that he took his architect's fee and gave half to the contractor and half to the client. Shortly after, on the way to the airport, Wright stopped by the house and, finding Carlson not at home, he took out a ball-point pen and wrote on the wood door, 'Hurrah for Ray', and signed it. Wright's apprentice Richard Carney called Carlson to apologize for what might be taken as vandalism, but Carlson said, 'I instantly recognized the signature and have already put a coat of shellac over the inscription to protect it!'[3]

A number of Wright's designs from this period exemplify the fact that, while at first glance the Usonians may appear formulaic, in fact they differ dramatically in response to site and client, so that in experience it can be said that no two are at all alike. The house in Phoenix Wright designed in 1951 for his old friend Benjamin Adelman, the owner of a laundry in Milwaukee, was one of the first of the 'Usonian Automatics', constructed of site-cast concrete blocks, both solid and glazed, and nestled into its desert landscape under the deep shadow of the concrete slab roof. The W. L. Fuller House, built in Pass Christian, Mississippi, in 1951, was sited on the coast of the Gulf of Mexico in a heavily wooded tidal flood zone. In an entirely uncharacteristic response to the coastal forest environment, Wright lifted the entire house up on columns, yet maintained the overall horizontal proportioning of the massing. This remarkable house was lost when the devastating 320 km/h (200 mph) winds of hurricane Camille struck the Gulf coast in 1969, killing more than 250 people. The Louis Penfield House (1952) was built in Willoughby Hills, Ohio, for a client who, in addition to being a public school art teacher, was 1.95 metres (6 ft 5 in) tall. In this elegantly crafted design, Wright adjusted his typical ceiling heights, creating dramatic vertical spaces at the stair and in the 3.66-metre (12 ft) tall living room.

It was also in this period that Wright and Mumford rekindled their relationship, when in 1951 Wright sent Mumford a copy of an exhibition catalogue inscribed, 'In spite of all, your old FLW'. Mumford recalls turning to his wife Sophie and saying,

I've just written a book in which I've said that without a great upsurgence of love we shall not be able to save the world from even greater orgies of extermination and destruction. If I haven't enough love left in me to answer Wright in the same fashion as this greeting, I'd better throw that book out the window.[4]

Mumford and Wright found common ground in their shared opposition to the communist 'witch-hunt' of Senator Joseph McCarthy's Committee on Un-American Activities, the cold war with Russia and China, the threat of nuclear annihilation, and the rise of the international bureaucracy of the United Nations. In 1949 Wright had supported the Cultural and Scientific Conference for World Peace, held in New York City; in 1950 he signed the World Peace Appeal; and in 1951 he supported the Emergency Civil Liberties Committee, set up to combat the loss of constitutional rights. In 1951 the Committee on Un-American Activities' list of Americans supposedly affiliated with communist-front organizations included Wright along with actors Jose Ferrer and Judy Holliday, singer Paul Robeson, authors Dashiell Hammett and Thomas Mann, playwright Lillian Hellman, composer Aaron Copland and physicist Albert Einstein.[5]

Wright, who was personally mortified that McCarthy was a senator from his home state of Wisconsin, attacked him directly, writing in 1951: 'I ask my fellow citizens . . . which is most dangerous to our Democratic system of free men: a sociological idiot like a Communist or a political pervert like McCarthy?' Wright went on to ask what Jesus 'would say of a Nation taking its children out of school on *suspicion* of aggression to make soldiers of them. Aggression *actual* is one thing. Aggression *imaginary* is quite another.' In a front page editorial of 22 September 1952 in *The Capital Times* of Madison, titled 'Wake Up, Wisconsin', Wright wrote: 'Our worst enemy now is this craven fear managed by conscienceless politicians . . . These fighters of communism! Do they really know what communism means? Ask them. Their answers will make you laugh. Do they know what democracy means? Ask them and weep.'[6]

In 1951 Wright wrote: 'Not only peace in Korea, the peace of the world, so it seems to me, would be best served if the United States of America would try to recover the lost art of minding its own business.' He went on to ask, 'Of what moral value to this world in agony is a United Nations composed of the "big three" imposing their will upon

the world and calling their will Freedom?'[7] In 1952 Wright attacked
the International Style, singling out the United Nations Building,
proposed for New York, as a particularly egregious example of mixing
bad architecture and bad politics. That same year Mumford wrote to
Wright that the UN building was 'cast in the image of automatism and
bureaucracy, and it is those twin agents, the mechanical function
and the mechanical functionary, both divorced from the subordinate
position they might occupy in the interests of life, that constitute
the real menace of our time.'

In 1953 Mumford reported to Wright that his speech at the
centennial celebration of the Cooper Union in New York was

> so full of challenging thoughts about the fear and suspicion and
> poisonous hatred and irrationality now rampant among our coun-
> trymen that not a word of it got into the newspapers. There is a sort
> of cold censorship at work that confirms and supports the mistakes
> of the cold war and the congealed minds that are waging it.

After Mumford wrote a 'The Sky Line' column attacking the UN
building, Wright wrote saying, 'Vive *The New Yorker*! What other
magazine would have dared? . . . Emerson would put his hand on
your shoulder and say, "my son".' Mumford responded by noting
that his columns often had to address subject matter

> too trivial to be worth the time one had to spend on it . . . But
> there are so few places left where it is possible to speak in a
> clean, straightforward fashion, with no regard for anything
> but clarity and truth, that I find myself holding on to the job
> as a sort of public duty.[8]

As had so often been the case in Wright's life up to this point, he
would at this moment be recognized once again by the Europeans –
the countries from which had come the classical and modern styles

against which he railed, yet also the cultures that seemed always more aware of his true importance to architecture than was his own. Since autumn 1949 Wright and his apprentices had been preparing the exhibition *Frank Lloyd Wright: Sixty Years of Living Architecture*, the idea for which had been conceived at the American Embassy in Rome, where the Ambassador, Clare Booth Luce, playwright and wife of publisher Henry Luce, and Arthur Kaufmann, of Gimbel Brothers department store in Pittsburgh, had been discussing ways to counteract the rise of communism in Italian politics. After the idea of an exhibit of creative works by Americans was proposed, Italian cultural figures were asked to suggest whose work should be selected, and their unanimous answer was 'Wright'.[9]

This was at least partly due to the influence of Bruno Zevi, the architectural historian and author of *Towards an Organic Architecture* (1945), the first architectural book to appear after the war; its one and only illustration, on the cover, was of Fallingwater. That same year Zevi also founded the Associazione per l'Architettura Organica, with chapters in nine major Italian cities. Wright's selection also indicates the manner in which his work had for some years been seen by Italians as diametrically opposed to fascism, beginning with Edoardo Persico's lecture in January 1935 in Turin, wherein he argued that Wright's work represented the best of the modern movement, embodying as it did the aspects of freedom, individuality and diversity in society. The antifascist movement in Italian architecture, led by Persico and Giuseppe Pagano, editor of *Casabella*, who died in a Nazi concentration camp, had come to see Wright's organic architecture as an idealized vision of life in a free society. Thus it is hardly coincidental that the primary organizer of Wright's exhibit in Italy was the art historian Carlo Ludovico Ragghianti, a legendary resistance fighter. In 1944, in order to maintain contact between the resistance forces in the city and the Allied troops on the other side of the Arno, Ragghianti had crossed Florence's Ponte Vecchio at dead of night, threading his way through the upper-level passageway, the Corridoio Vasariano, which had been mined by the Germans.[10]

There was another, even more important European connection for Wright's *Sixty Years of Living Architecture* exhibit – the architect and sculptor Oscar Stonorov, who organized the exhibition and accompanied it on its entire three-year tour. Stonorov, a German-born architect whose father was Russian and mother was French, had worked briefly for Le Corbusier and was an editor for the first volume of Le Corbusier's *Œuvre complete* (Zürich, 1930). Stonorov, with his partner Alfred Kastner, received second prize in the 1931 Palace of the Soviets international competition, and subsequently designed and built one of the very first union workers' housing blocks in the US, the Carl Mackley Houses (1932–5) in Philadelphia. From 1941 to 1947 he was Louis Kahn's partner in Philadelphia, where Stonorov's union connections and political activism resulted in the firm's receiving significant public housing work, and he was later appointed director of the Philadelphia Housing Association. In 1949 Stonorov was retained by the Gimbel family of Philadelphia to work on Wright's exhibit, and the Russian-German émigré soon become close friends with Wright and Oglivanna. Stonorov even attempted to sculpt a bust of Wright's head, intended for the exhibit – an effort that was ultimately thwarted by the Wrights' incessant nocturnal modifications.

Sixty Years of Living Architecture was the largest exhibit of Wright's work ever mounted, and likely the largest to date of any single architect in history. It consisted of hundreds of large photographic murals, decorative objects, more than a thousand original drawings and renderings, and twenty-eight models, as well as the twelve-foot-square Broadacre City model. The exhibit premiered in January 1951 in Philadelphia at Gimbel's Department Store; Frederick Gimbel would eventually donate $50,000 to sponsor the tour, including a stipend for Stonorov's organization of the exhibit. The exhibit's international tour was sponsored by the US government, and Wright wrote special introductions for each of the exhibit's venues, starting with one for the Philadelphia schoolchildren who came to the exhibit

From left to right, Oglivanna Wright, Frank Lloyd Wright, Bruno Zevi, Carlo Ludovico Ragghianti, Count Carlo Sforza, Oscar Stonorov, overlooking Broadacre City model in Florence, 1951.

by the hundreds, and followed by personal notes addressed to Italy, Switzerland, France, Germany, Netherlands, Mexico and the US, where the exhibition would also be shown in New York and Los Angeles. Over the next two years Wright would travel to Italy, France and Mexico for the openings of this exhibition, which he believed would be his last.

In 1951 Wright, along with Oglivanna and their daughter Iovanna, travelled to Italy, arriving in Rome and then going to Assisi, where Wright studied the frescoes then attributed to Giotto in the monastery of San Francesco. After a brief overview of the exhibit, installed in the Doge's Palace in Florence, Wright then travelled to Venice, where in a solemn ceremony in the Doge's Palace he received an honorary degree from the University of Venice, as well as the Star of Solidarity, one of Italy's highest awards. In Venice Wright was met by crowds of students, as his work was of the utmost importance to the school of architecture, directed by Giuseppe Samona and with Carlo Scarpa a leader of the design faculty. Zevi recalled, 'When Wright walked in the *calli* or through the *piazzette*, or when he traveled by gondola, Venetians of all social strata recognized, greeted, and applauded him.' During a visit to the Venini glass factory on Murano, Wright selected six glass objects to purchase – every one of which, it turned out, was designed by Carlo Scarpa. Wright next visited Rome, where Zevi took him to see the architecture of the Baroque master of light and space, Francesco Borromini.[11] The Wrights then went on to the opening of the exhibit in Florence, where, in one of the events of his life he most cherished, Wright received the De' Medici Gold Medal in the Palazzo Vecchio, making him an honorary citizen of Florence.

The most controversial event inspired by the exhibit would occur in Italy, where Angelo Masieri, a 30-year-old architect and former student of Scarpa, asked Wright to design a replacement for his house, at the corner of the Grand Canal and Rio Nuovo next to the Palazzo Balbi and facing the Ca' Foscari. In 1952 Masieri and his wife Savina came to the US to visit Wright's works and discuss the project with him, but during the trip Masieri was tragically killed in an automobile accident. Savina Masieri and the school of architecture of Venice, with Scarpa as their representative, then commissioned Wright to design a residence and study centre for architecture students on the Masieri house site on the Grand Canal, to be called the Masieri Memorial Foundation. Wright's design, despite being an elegant and uncharacteristically restrained abstraction of the typical Venetian palazzo, nevertheless ignited a fierce international debate between those who maintained that Venice should remain a museum, untouched by modern building, and those who insisted that, in order to survive, Venice must be as a living, evolving city. Bernard Berenson, the distinguished Italian Renaissance art historian and long-time resident of Florence, opposed the project, as did Wright's fellow Oak Park resident Ernest Hemingway, who said that if Wright's design was built Venice deserved to be burned. Wright retorted, 'A voice from the jungle.'[12] The international outcry, as well as pressure from the Venetian Tourist Commission, eventually forced the city to reject Wright's design. More than twenty years later Scarpa would realize the Masieri Foundation by removing the interior walls and floors of the original palazzo, leaving the historic outer wall as a shell, within which entirely modern spaces were constructed.

In May 1952, Wright launched yet another attack on the International Style in his *Architectural Record* essay 'Organic Architecture Looks at Modern Architecture', ridiculing Mies van der Rohe's motto, '"Less is more" unless less, already little, becomes less than nothing at all and "much ado about nothing"', claiming that modern architecture was organic architecture 'deprived of a soul', and holding that 'any "international style" would probably be a cultural calamity fit for Fascism but intolerable for democracy.'[13] The stridency of Wright's rhetoric suggests that at this time, in the midst of the Korean War, which he vehemently opposed, as he had the previous two World Wars, and with the International Style becoming increasingly dominant in American corporate architecture, he was feeling very much the dishonoured prophet in his own country – a voice crying in the wilderness.

Thus the April 1953 essay in the William Randolph Hearst family publication *House Beautiful*, written by its editor, Elizabeth Gordon, criticizing the International Style as inappropriate for America, came like a beacon in the night. Wright fired off a telegram to Gordon, saying, 'I didn't know you had it in you. I am at your service from now on', signed 'The Godfather'.[14] Noting the telegram's Spring Green origination, Gordon contacted Wright and this marked the start of a short but mutually beneficial relationship, with *House Beautiful* repeatedly publishing Wright's works, and with four of Wright's apprentices eventually working for the magazine, most notably John deKoven Hill, who became the architecture editor. In October of that same year *House Beautiful* published Wright's essay 'For a Democratic Architecture', in which he responded to the statement from a group of San Francisco Bay area architects that architecture was not primarily concerned with social or political meanings. In November 1955 the entire 385-page issue of *House Beautiful* was dedicated to Wright's domestic works.

House Beautiful and all the other publications and news media by which Wright reached his national and international audiences were based in New York City – the other great 'nemesis' whose recognition he craved. Wright's complex and contradictory love-hate relationship with the Big Apple was the subject of Herbert Muchamp's 1983 book-length study *Man About Town*, in which Muchamp noted that, while in the 1920s Wright had fled to New York to escape the press, in the 1950s he came to New York to seek publicity. He had long ago developed close and supportive relationships with the New York-based publishers, editors and writers at *Architectural Record*, the Luce publications *Architectural Forum*, *Fortune*, *Time* and *Life*, as well as *The Nation*, *The New Republic* and, of course, his favourite, *The New Yorker*, on whose staff were Woollcott and Mumford. In 1953 Wright signed an exclusive contract with a new publisher, Horizon Press, also based in New York, and they would publish a new Wright book every year from 1953 to 1959.

It was during this period, with an increasing number of commissions in the metropolitan New York area, that Wright formalized his 'home and office' in the city. Wright had been using the Plaza Hotel, at the corner of Fifth Avenue and 59th Street (Central Park South), as his headquarters while visiting the city since his trip to Europe in 1909, and with ever increasing frequency since the late 1930s. In 1953 Wright rented Plaza Hotel Suite 223 on a permanent basis, setting about renovating the space he claimed once belonged to Diamond Jim Brady. He installed plum-coloured velvet curtains from ceiling to floor, peach-coloured wool carpet, wall panels of gold Japanese paper, circular mirrors, simple black-lacquered, red-edged furniture of his own design (fabricated by the apprentices at Taliesin West), and a selection of his oriental art objects.

Situated on the north-east corner of the second floor, with views of Central Park and Fifth Avenue, the suite at the Plaza, where Wright spent an increasing amount of his time during his last six years, had been christened 'Taliesin the Third' by Howard Meyers, editor of *Architectural Forum*, several years before it became permanent. Frederick Gutheim, Wright's editor for his 1941 collection of essays, recalled having breakfast with Wright at Taliesin the Third 'on several occasions, looking across at Central Park, and [Wright's] complaints were endless – including the rancid butter.' Wright's sister Maginel Wright Barney, a long-time New York City resident and the Wrights' host in 1927, was regularly asked by Wright to bring baked potatoes and baked ham to the Plaza, which she had to smuggle in through the lobby in a brown paper bag – home-cooked food that Wright and Oglivanna consumed, skins and all.[15]

Solomon Guggenheim, Wright's original patron for the Guggenheim Museum, had also had a suite at the Plaza Hotel, and Wright's Plaza suite was just down Fifth Avenue from the museum site at 88th Street. In 1951 Hilla Rebay had been driven from her position as director of the Guggenheim Collection by intense criticism, including a lengthy Sunday *New York Times* article by the art critic Aline Saarinen, wife of Eliel Saarinen's son Eero. James Sweeney, a close friend of Alvar Aalto, was named the new director. From the start he was not supportive of Wright's design and rejected Rebay's original vision of the collection being 'frozen' so as to consist of only 'non-objective' works. As Wright noted, without the support of Harry Guggenheim, who had taken control of the project at Solomon's death, and his decision to put the family's wealth squarely behind the building, Wright's design would never have been realized.

The Guggenheim Museum site, at the end of a full 200-foot city block facing Central Park, had finally been secured in 1951, but several years later the building bureaucracy of New York City was still proving obstructive. As Wright's cousin Robert Moses recalled in his speech at the museum's dedication ceremony, Wright's 'battle with the city department of buildings is famous wherever inspiration clashes with bureaucracy. The commissioner of buildings has to live by the book, and Commissioner Gillroy tossed the book at cousin Frank.' Moses, in a move that indicates the very real affection and respect between him and Wright, called the building commissioner, saying, 'I will have a building permit on my desk by 8.00 am tomorrow or there will be a new building commissioner.' The permit was delivered, but construction on the Guggenheim Museum did not begin until 1956, and Wright would not live to see it completed. Moses's continued ambivalence towards Wright's museum and its collection is clear in the conclusion to his speech: 'If I cannot honestly say I comprehend all that goes on here, I can admire hospitality to new ideas, for it is only the open mind which insures progress.'[16]

In 1953 the Guggenheim Museum's Fifth Avenue site was occupied by two temporary structures of Wright's design: the pavilion to house the exhibition *Sixty Years of Living Architecture*, recently returned from Mexico, and a full-size Usonian House. The Usonian House was built by David Henken, contractor for the Usonian Houses that had been built at 'Usonia' in Pleasantville, New York. With its floor-to-ceiling glass doors in the tall living room, its ceiling constructed of square plywood panel ceilings, its lower ceiling forming intimate alcoves along two sides of the room, and its massive masonry fireplace, the house formed a highly dynamic spatial composition.

The main exhibition pavilion, constructed using simple scaffolding technology, formed a 30–60–90-degree roof and wall plane of translucent panels, the lighting effect of which was quite similar to Taliesin West. In one of Pedro Guerrero's informal photographs of Wright in the pavilion before the exhibit opened, we see the architect sitting before the photomurals of the Larkin Building, and there is just a touch of sadness in his gaze. The Larkin Building, one of Wright's greatest works, had been demolished by the city of Buffalo the year before, for no apparent reason: to this day the empty site remains overgrown with weeds and is not even used as a parking lot.

Mumford, who had long intended to write an extended evaluation of Wright's lifework, found his opportunity with the opening of the New York exhibition of 1953. Mumford's two-part article in *The New Yorker*, titled 'A Phoenix Too Infrequent', began by stating that the 86-year-old Wright was not only America's greatest architect, but 'one of the most creative architectural geniuses of all time'. Yet

Mumford went on to express concern not only with what he felt was Wright's imposition of his design 'ego' on all aspects of the clients' lives, reflecting Mumford's brief stay in the Hanna House, and his reaction to its trapezoid-shaped beds and special linens, but also with his architectural isolationism – 'the America First streak in Wright is a coarse, dark vein in the fine granite of his mind' – which Mumford felt hindered the full development of Modern architecture. Mumford ended his two articles with what he and Wright shared:

> The fact remains that in a period of specialist constrictions and nationalist conformities his lifework has expressed the full gamut of *human* scale, from mathematics to poetry, from pure form to pure feeling, from the regional to the planetary, from the personal to the cosmic. In an age intimidated by its successes and depressed by a series of disasters, he awakens, by his still confident example, a sense of the fullest *human* possibilities.

What most dismayed Mumford was the reaction of those who came to view the exhibit: 'Wright's exhibition has puzzled visitors . . . [because] many of Wright's most audacious innovations have been generally absorbed during the last half-century.' In particular the Usonian House, with what Mumford called its 'almost old-fashioned, homey air', was perplexing to those who attended, for what was the point of erecting what appeared to most uninformed observers to be a typical suburban 'ranch' house on Fifth Avenue? The fact that the house's open floor plan, extensive glazing and sunlight, integrated indirect lighting, built-in storage and furnishings, central open kitchen, living and dining combined in one room, plywood panelling, corner brick fireplace, exposed materials and modular construction had all originated with Wright, and were his legacy for America – now completely integrated into typical single-family house planning – was something about which the average citizen of the time was evidently blissfully ignorant.[17]

Wright did not take Mumford's criticism at all well, particularly what he called the 'insults' to his clients and himself implied in the charge that he willfully imposed his designs on his clients. He responded that his clients themselves had answered that charge, through the hundreds of letters he had received from them, telling how their houses had dramatically changed their lives for the better. Mumford wrote back to Wright that 'the best praise of a man's work is not that which is unqualified, but that which remains after all qualifications.' The exchange ended, and all was forgiven, with a pair of insightful remarks that all writers on architecture would do well to take to heart: Wright stated, 'Literature tells what happens to man, but Architecture presents him', to which Mumford replied, 'As for your work, it will remain long after anything I write about it and will have the last word. That is as it should be.'[18]

Twenty three years after its original conception, Wright finally realized a design directly related in both plan and section to his seminal St Mark's Tower when he built the H. C. Price Company Tower in Bartlesville, Oklahoma, in 1952. The Price Tower stands alone on the prairie, as Wright intended towers to be located in his larger Broadacre City plan. The Price Tower was built for Harold Price, a wealthy oil and natural gas pipeline builder who also built two houses of Wright's design: his own in Bartlesville (1953), and a house for his mother in Paradise Valley, Arizona, in 1954. The Price family, true patrons of Modern architecture, would go on in later years to commission houses from Bruce Goff and Steven Holl. The Price Tower contains eight double-height apartments in one quadrant of the square plan, with single-height offices taking up the other three quadrants of each floor, and abandons the hanging curtain wall of the St Marks prototype by expressing the concrete floor slabs folding up at the outer edge, with the copper-clad windows set between them to give the vertical tower a horizontal rhythm. Wright used this same detail in his 1953 design for the

Point View Tower, an apartment building in Pittsburgh, the penthouse of which was intended for Edgar Kaufmann, but which, like all of Wright's many projects commissioned by Kaufmann for Pittsburgh, was not to be realized.

The last decade of Wright's life brought him several opportunities to realize designs he had made in the 1920s, including the 1926 Steel Cathedral, which Wright employed as the starting point for his design of the Beth Sholom Synagogue, built in Elkins Park, Pennsylvania, in 1954. The synagogue is triangular in plan, its base a solid-walled, concrete vessel set into the earth, and its top a woven crystalline roof allowing light to fall into the space from above. The congregation's rabbi, Mortimer Cohen, had asked Wright to design a building that incorporated elements of both American and Jewish experience, and the synagogue's three steel legs supporting the steeply inclined woven walls of metal, glass and plastic may be related to both the tepee tents of Native Americans and the 'traveling Mount Sinai' requested by Cohen – the 'mountain of light' where Moses received the Torah from God during the time the Israelites wandered in the desert. With its protective enclosure below and glowing roof above, the Beth Sholom Synagogue is a powerful demonstration of Wright's unmatched capacity to translate ritual into inhabited space and experience.

In late 1954, partly as a result of anonymous allegations and continuous FBI investigations of both the Taliesin Fellowship, a school receiving funding under the GI Bill, and Wright himself – largely provoked by his public stands against the cold war and McCarthyism – the state supreme court of Wisconsin declared that Taliesin was an architectural office, not a school, and therefore it did not qualify for tax-exempt status, handing Wright a bill for almost $19,000 in back taxes. The local newspapers came to his defence, pointing to the numerous *pro bono* designs he had offered Wisconsin, including his Butterfly Bridges. In an indication of his changing attitude towards the Big Apple, Wright threatened to burn Taliesin to the ground and move his practice to New York City. A dinner was quickly organized, attended by the governor and hundreds of dignitaries, and funds were raised to pay the Taliesin Fellowship's tax bill.

Wright's image as a political and social rebel continued to cost him dearly, even in this period of unparalleled productivity. In 1954 the national government sponsored a competition to design the Air Force Academy in Colorado Springs; after considering the proposals, the finalists were announced as Wright and Skidmore, Owings and Merrill, a New York 'plan factory' (as Wright called large corporate offices) and disciples of Mies van der Rohe. The American Legion, involved in the architect selection process, threatened to make a public protest if Wright's design was chosen, and Wright was forced to withdraw. These events were not revealed until more than a year later, when *Architectural Forum* noted that all it took for the American Legion to kill Wright's design was their threat to dredge up Wright's anti-war activities, which being 'front-paged for America in its 1955 mood' would have made it impossible for the Air Force to select him.[19]

Wright was spending ever more time in New York City, and his suite was often used as a drafting room, where numerous ex-apprentices who lived and worked in New York would come in to work on projects. Edgar Tafel, who at this point had established a well-respected practice in New York, recalled receiving telephone calls from Wright inquiring as to whether Tafel was available to run out and get some blueprints made, leading Tafel to remark: 'We apprentices never advanced beyond the age at which [Wright had] first met us.' Another former apprentice, Bob Mosher, had taken a position with a large New York contractor, and his firm was asked to bid on the Guggenheim Museum in 1955. Mosher brought the plans to Tafel's office, where they were seen by Tafel's friend George Cohen, a concrete contractor, who tried unsuccessfully to get on the bidding list. Six weeks later Tafel received a call from Wright at 7.00 am on a Saturday morning, reporting that the lowest bids for the museum had come in at twice the budget, and telling Tafel to send 'his concrete man' over to the

Plaza Hotel immediately. When Cohen visited Wright at his suite that morning, Wright greeted him, 'So you are the expert in concrete?' to which Cohen replied, 'No, Mr Wright, I have come to learn from you.' Wright's delighted response: 'You are my man.' Cohen built the museum within the budget, and he and Wright became fast friends. As the building went up, Cohen proposed a cornerstone, to which Wright replied, 'A round building doesn't have a cornerstone, George.'[20]

In December 1956, as the Guggenheim Museum was under construction, 21 New York painters, including Franz Kline, Willem de Kooning, Milton Avery, Philip Guston, Adolf Gottlieb and Robert Motherwell, delivered to the museum's trustees a petition criticizing Wright's design. The artists held that Wright's spiraling ramp compared unfavourably with the traditional white rectangular box as a place to display Modern art. Wright expressed considerable amusement at what he characterized as the architectural and spatial conservatism of these self-proclaimed avant-garde artists, and their desire to continue to subject their paintings to what he called 'the strait jacket of the tyrannical rectilinear', despite the Modern liberation of space. Wright believed that Modern art, which purported to represent space and form in a new, fully integrated manner, would be most appropriately displayed inside exactly such a Modern plastic space as he had designed: 'a new unity between beholder, painting and architecture', taking place in ever-changing natural light, which brought awareness of the time of day and season of the year.[21]

Wright, of course, would have the last word in this debate: today not only is the Guggenheim Museum enormously popular with the public, but his design is credited by many artists with engendering profound reinterpretations of the perceived boundaries and bonds between Modern painting, sculpture and architecture. The artists' protest may in the end have had more to do with their apprehension that Wright's Guggenheim Museum itself was destined to become

Wright leaning against wall on roof of the Guggenheim Museum, New York, photograph taken during construction, with spiralling walls behind Wright.

the greatest work of art in the collection, one result of which is that 'picture postcards of the building have always outsold those depicting its collection'.[22]

In 1957 Andy Rooney, later a commentator on the CBS news programme 'Sixty Minutes', recalled collecting Wright at the Plaza for a television interview. As Rooney drove to the CBS studio in Grand Central Station, he remembered Wright complaining about everything in New York. In order to access the studio, they had to ascend in an elevator and walk across one of the steel and glass catwalks suspended between the two layers of glazing in the large, arched windows opening between the city outside and the train station's 38-metre (125 ft) high main waiting room – one of the greatest spaces in New York City. Wright said, 'It's a grand building, isn't it?' Then, as Rooney recalled: 'Midway across, Wright stopped [on the glass catwalk] and neither of us said anything. He must have stood there for more than five minutes, and I didn't speak because I knew nothing I had to say could match what he was thinking.'[23]

That same year Wright gave among his greatest performances in 'The Mike Wallace Interviews', taped in New York at the same CBS studio in Grand Central Station. Wallace would later call these 'two of the most challenging and enlightening interviews I've ever done.' Wallace opened the first interview by stating that Wright was America's 'foremost social rebel' and 'social critic', and asking about his views on war, to which Wright replied he was 'against war, always have been, always will be'. Despite his reputation to the contrary, he stated that he was not 'against cities', but was rather 'against congestion'. Wright attacked the conformist 'mobocracy', but, when Wallace asked if today's young people were not also a mob, Wright said no, that he believed in the youth of America. When asked about the accusations that he was anti-American, Wright fired back: 'Is there anything more anti-American than McCarthyism?' At the end of the first interview, Wallace closed by calling Wright the leading 'nonconformist in an age of conformism', to which Wright interjected, 'Mike, am I listening to my own epitaph?', making Wallace laugh.

Wallace recalled that, at the end of the first interview, there was so much left to discuss that they taped an unprecedented second interview. Wright opened by stating that, even today, 'we do not understand what it is to live in a natural house', holding that 'architecture should grace the landscape, not be a disgrace', and that 'we are not a culture, we are only a civilization'. Countering Mumford's criticism, Wright noted the hundreds of letters he had received from clients telling how their life had been changed for the better. Pressed about his positive statements on the Russians in the 1930s, Wright said 'the government in Russia is a kind of gangsterism – and here too, lately', pointedly bringing the discussion back to the US. Wright asked, 'Where is there today a group of people who understand the Declaration of Independence and the responsibilities it places upon them?' Wright held that Americans 'have not gone to school to learn the nature of things', and that without such training we were always in danger of losing our democracy. Wright maintained that, in his ninth decade, he was 'more rebellious now, but more quiet about it. If your work is good and right, it will defend you.' Asked by Wallace if he was afraid of death, Wright immediately said, 'Not at all . . . [Being] young has no meaning, you can do nothing about it. Youth is a quality, and if you have it you never lose it.'[24]

As Gutheim would later recall,

> It requires an effort to appreciate Wright's age . . . He should have been a Victorian; but he did not belong to that culture. To me he was detached from any chronological definition; he stood alone. But that means he found it easy to relate to contemporaries as he found them at any point in time. It was one reason for his success with the youth – of any time.[25]

Yet it was Wright's youthfulness, his ability to connect instantly with young people, noted by so many observers, and the spontaneous quality of youth that had begun at this time to disappear from the daily lives of the young people of the Taliesin Fellowship. The term most often used to describe post-Second World War Taliesin is 'cult', and that was with good reason. Although Gurdjieff died in 1949, he had made a number of extended visits to Taliesin, starting in the 1930s; he considered Oglivanna his chief disciple; Wright's daughter Iovanna had gone to Fontainebleau to study with Gurdjieff in 1948. This mesmerizing mystic's influence was palpably present at Taliesin during this period.

The increasingly ritualistic daily life at Taliesin had long been guided by Oglivanna, who effectively assumed the guise of high priestess. Oglivanna had become more and more dictatorial in the everyday lives of the apprentices and their spouses, requiring all to reveal to her the intimate details of their private lives, and often being accused of trying to break up marriages by arranging affairs between those she thought better matched. Every aspect of the apprentices' life – dress, daily work duties, meals, social life and normally private matters – was subject to Oglivanna's ceaseless control and masterful manipulation. In a sign of the ever-more undemocratic nature of Taliesin, Wright and his family now took all their meals on the raised dias, whereas before they had only listened to Sunday concerts from that superior position. Apprentices recall Wright occasionally protesting loudly to Oglivanna that he was not going to have Taliesin turn into 'one of those Gurdjieff cults', but his wife had long ago learned how to distract and redirect him.

Far more troubling was the effect this cult-like atmosphere began to have on Wright's designs. At Taliesin Wright had been surrounded for 25 years by those who literally worshipped him, and constructive criticism had disappeared altogether. The effect of his increasingly isolated situation (physically, socially, intellectually), the vast amount of work coming into the office, and the absolute ban Oglivanna imposed on any kind of criticism of his ideas – no matter how far-fetched they might be – led inevitably to a decline in the quality of many of Wright's designs. In 1934 Wright's friend John Dewey had written: 'Time is the test that discriminates the imaginative from the imaginary. The latter passes because it is arbitrary. The imaginative endures because, while at first strange with respect to us, it is enduringly familiar with respect to the nature of things.'[26] During this period Wright often seems to have lost his innate grasp of the imaginative, as Dewey defined it, falling instead into the realm of the purely imaginary – abandoning the poetic for the preposterous.

Every sketch from Wright's hand was now, by definition, a stroke of genius. Apprentices recall Wright, after dashing off a drawing at his board, saying to himself, *sotto voce* but still loud enough so all could hear, 'I'm a genius this morning.' Genius of this sort does not feel compelled to explain itself, nor is it accountable or responsible to anything except its own whims. Wright could not have avoided being affected by the ritualized lifestyle that developed around him at Taliesin, where he was the centre of all attention, revered almost as a god. However, it is also certain that architecture of quality cannot emerge in the absence of constructive criticism – whether self-criticism or the criticism of respected colleagues. As a result, the integration of space, function, construction, human scale and landscape that had always been Wright's unifying and primary principle of design now began to disappear from his work, and a kind of disintegration began to dominate many of his larger designs.

Wright's designs of this late period often registered this disintegration in the distance they became removed from those very aspects that Wright earlier considered fundamental to his architecture. The Kalita Humphries Theater (1955), built in Dallas, Texas, is a concrete mass with almost no sense of scale, either material or human, and its interior is subjected to a dictatorial geometry that results in such things as trapezoidal stairs that threaten their users with an almost certain tumble. In the unbuilt project for the V. C. Morris House of 1955, proposed for an incredible site in San Francisco overlooking the Pacific Ocean, Wright's intuitive sense of the minimal needed to achieve maximum richness of experience is abandoned as the diminutive house was poised atop an enormous, multi-storeyed, telescoping concrete abutment, which appears absurdly exaggerated when we recall the subtle yet powerful buttresses lurking in the shadows under Fallingwater. The Annunciation Greek Orthodox Church, designed in 1956 but not completed until 1962, is perhaps Wright's most geometrically pure and precise floor plan, yet the circular form and elliptical section, complete with decorative arches edging the roof, suggest a building that is lifting off the ground – looking like nothing so much as a flying saucer – and thereby losing the anchorage in the earth so important to Wright's architecture. The 1957 project for a house for playwright Arthur Miller and his wife Marilyn Monroe called for a enormous concrete dome roof to be placed atop a series of stone-clad, cylindrical columns – a structural 'collision' that indicates Wright's loss of his intuitive sense of the experiential presence of structural forms. Needless to say, Miller rejected the overwrought and overly expensive project, and all that Wright seems to have taken away from this debacle was his quip to Mike Wallace that Marilyn Monroe was 'very good architecture'. In the Donohue 'Triptych' House project of 1959, designed for Paradise Valley, Arizona, Wright's intention was to 'put the top back onto the mountain' – *on* the hill, not *of* it – a complete reversal of his previous principles, exemplified in his sensitive nestling of Taliesin around the brow of its hill. The Grady Grammage Auditorium, built at Arizona State University in 1959, is a cylindrical volume surrounded by a structurally unnecessary line of ludicrously thin columns supporting puffy sagging arches, indicating the total absence of Wright's heretofore characteristic ability to experientially ground the inhabitants of his buildings through the manner in which they were constructed. Wright, it appears, had all but forgotten his own definition of 1949: 'the art of building wherein aesthetic and construction *not only approve but prove each other.*'[27]

Perhaps the most disappointing design from Wright's late period – because its initial conception held such wonderful promise – is the Marin County Civic Center, designed in 1957 and completed after Wright's death. When Wright first visited the steeply rolling, grass and oak tree-covered hills in Northern California, the client indicated the hills could be flattened to accommodate the building. Wright immediately replied, 'To the contrary, those hills will be the feature of the design, and the building will be a bridge between them.' The building does bridge from hilltop to hilltop as a series of long bars, pivoting around the circular council chamber, yet the aqueduct-like forms are faced in stacked layers of non-structural arches, hung off the concrete floor slab behind, completely destroying any sense of structural reality. The focal feature of the design is not the public space of assembly, but rather the tall triangular radio and television broadcast tower – a disturbing realization of Wright's prediction, opposed by both Dewey and Mumford, that the various forms of electronic media would render the public realm of face-to-face meetings obsolete and unnecessary in the suburban redefinition of American democracy.

By far the most uncharacteristic design of Wright's later years was his Mile High Tower of 1956, designed for his beloved Chicago, 1,609 metres (5,280 ft, i.e. 1 mile) and 528 floors tall, its taproot foundation extending as far into the earth below as the Empire State Building rose into the sky above: the drawing for the building itself was more than 6.7 metres (22 ft) long. In an absurd argument for such a design, Wright claimed that only three Mile High Towers, sited in Central Park, would be necessary to replace all the density of New York City, thereby calling his entire Broadacre City proposal into question. Yet, even though Wright felt that this design placed him in the realm of the great builders of modern times, his Mile High was destined never to be realized, not because it was unbuildable – for it was technically within the realm of possibility – but because Wright presented it as a purely abstract exercise in publicity, not conceiving it as he had his other high-rise designs, as a place scaled and ordered for human experience.

The Mile High Tower would also cause the final split between Mumford and Wright. The city of Chicago declared 17 October 1956 to be 'Frank Lloyd Wright Day' and, after his cousin Robert Moses was unable to chair the celebration, Wright asked Mumford to preside over the banquet. Mumford declined, however, believing that the event was intended primarily to publicize the Mile High Tower design, a project of which Mumford later wrote,

all of Wright's egocentric weaknesses were crystallized in an ultimate fantasy, conceived as if by a lineal descendant of Kublai Khan . . . Naturally, I could not lend myself to a proposal that violated every canon of Wright's own conception of an organic architecture, as well as my own. If this was what old age had done to Wright, I had no desire to exalt his mummified remains.[28]

As if to confirm Mumford's diagnosis, in 1958 Wright published *The Living City*, the text of which was simply recycled from his two earlier books on Broadacre City, *The Disappearing City* and *When Democracy Builds*. By this time it was becoming apparent to many observers that there was an inherent contradiction between Wright's careful planning and design of Broadacre City and his statements that Broadacre City would emerge spontaneously; be 'everywhere and nowhere'; not be recognizable as a city at all, in the traditional sense; and that 'America needs no help to Broadacre City; it will haphazardly build itself.' In a way similar to how the Usonian House had been absorbed into the suburban vernacular as the ubiquitous 'ranch' house, Broadacre City was haphazardly building itself as the endless sprawling development everywhere overtaking the American landscape. Wright's ambivalence towards what was in fact an appalling distortion of his ideas is indicated by the story Alvar Aalto told of driving through the suburbs of Boston in the 1950s with Wright, who waved towards the sprawl of houses, gas stations and roadside markets, saying, 'All this I have made possible.' While we might still be able to detect the faintest hint of self-deprecating irony in this remark, Aalto said later, 'I just couldn't see it.'[29]

Like the hero of Robert Heinlein's 1961 science fiction classic *Stranger in a Strange Land* – a human born and raised on Mars who returns to earth to find himself a kind of ghost in the machine of a society to which he is alien in every conceivable way, excepting only biological fact – Wright, to the last a Jeffersonian, railed against big government even as he demanded that same big government intervene to stop the Army Corps of Engineers from running electrical power lines through the desert, and to stop the haphazard encroachment of suburban sprawl from Scottsdale, both of which, by the late 1950s, were rapidly spoiling the panoramas of what was intended to be Wright's cultured retreat from civilization, Taliesin West.

Yet far and away the largest number of designs Wright realized in his last years were Usonian Houses, and 'the Usonian House, in all its guises, remains even now the last serious attempt on the part of an American architect to render the suburb a place of cultivation.'[30] Through his designs for the Usonian Houses, Wright was to the end endeavouring to reach out to the American public. This is exemplified by his outpouring of articles during the 1950s presenting his ideas, free of charge for anyone who wished to employ them, in homemaker and homebuilder magazines such as *House Beautiful*, *House and Garden*, *House and Home* and *Life*. In this revelation of his design 'secrets' to the public at large, Wright was almost alone among his profession, yet, as we have seen, he had consistently communicated directly with American families since the very beginning of his career.

House and Home, the Luce publication that gave Wright repeated coverage in this period, was addressed to the homemaker, contractor and home-builder, and four of its issues can be cited as examples of typical publications by Wright from this period: the September 1956 article on the Zimmerman House, built in Manchester, New Hampshire, was titled '32 Simple and Basic Design Ideas of Frank Lloyd Wright'; the December 1956 on the Marshall Erdman Company prefabricated houses designed by Wright was titled 'How Frank Lloyd Wright Designs for Prefabrication'; and the March 1958 and February 1959 articles on Lamberson and Alsop Houses built in Oslaloosa, Iowa, which document the fact that Wright's designs drew 9,000 visitors when completed. The last of these, based on an interview with the contractor and his crew, was titled 'Builder Jim De Reus Tells You: "What We Learned from Frank Lloyd Wright"'.

Over his final 25 years Wright designed hundreds of Usonian Houses, and they stand today as the only built indication of the ideals embodied in his Broadacre City and Usonia. These amazing houses were characterized by both astonishing quality of interior space and intimate relations to courtyard gardens, and they set a standard that has never been matched by the universally similar and experientially vacuous 'developer' products that have typified the American home-building industry since Wright's death. In *The Natural House* (1954), perhaps his most straightforward and sincere writing, Wright noted:

> What is needed most in architecture today is the very thing that is needed most in life – Integrity. Just as it is in a human being, so integrity is the deepest quality in a building; but it is a quality not so much demanded of any building since very ancient times when it was natural. It is no longer the first demand for a human being either, because 'Success' is now so immediately necessary . . . The Usonian House, then, aims to be a natural performance, one that is integral to site; integral to environment; integral to the life of the inhabitants.[31]

Wright suffered a stroke in 1958, and cataracts obscured his eyesight in his last years. But Wright's vision for American architecture, one that would nurture democracy, remained clear, as exemplified by the final writings he was working on at the time of his death: 'A Culture of Our Own', published in *Progressive* magazine in 1959, and his introduction to his proposed book for children, *The Wonderful World of Architecture*. Wright's faith in the Usonian House is also exemplified by the fact that the last project on his drawing board was not a resort or museum or civic centre, but a simple and affordable prefabricated concrete-block house for his friend Marshall Erdman's construction company.

At the Easter celebration at Taliesin West in April 1959, Wright's granddaughter, the actress Anne Baxter (who credited him with inspiring her career by designing her a theatre when she was three years old), recalled that Wright 'walked with small panther-smooth steps, the most graceful man I ever knew.'[32] Many have noted that Wright, though approaching his 92nd

Wright funeral procession, with Taliesin in the background.

year, still carried himself with remarkable dignity, agility, poise and elegance. Thus it came as a shock to all when, only a few days after the Easter party, Wright fell ill and was admitted to hospital in Phoenix. He was operated on for a intestinal obstruction, but after a valiant recovery he died on 9 April 1959.

Wright's son-in-law, Wes Peters, drove the body back to Wisconsin, 2,900 kilometres (1,800 miles) in 28 hours. On the evening of 12 April, Wright's casket, lined with Cherokee red velvet, was placed on a wagon heaped high with wildflowers and drawn by two black horses. The funeral procession of hundreds followed Wright's body as it was carried down the hill, through the double line of 150 cedar trees Wright had recently planted with the landscape architect Robert Graves, to the little Unity Chapel in the Valley, the first building upon which he had worked as an eighteen-year-old. Graves remembered that when they had finished planting the trees earlier that year, Wright turned to him and said, '"Taliesin is now finished", and I was overwhelmed. It seemed a terrible thing for him to say.'[33] Wright was buried in the shade of the old oak trees that surround Unity Chapel, next to his grandparents, his aunts and uncles, his mother, and his beloved Mamah Borthwick. Learning of Wright's death, Mies van der Rohe spoke for many when he said, 'In his undiminishing power he resembles a giant tree in a wide landscape which year after year attains a more noble crown.'[34]

With anyone but Frank Lloyd Wright, this would be the end of the story. But in death, as in life, it seemed Wright was doomed to be ever surrounded by scandal and controversy. Today this is discovered by anyone visiting Wright's grave at Unity Chapel in Spring Green, Wisconsin, for they find it empty. On 1 March 1985, almost 26 years after Wright's death, Oglivanna died in Scottsdale, Arizona. Her last wish before dying, though never mentioned in her will, was that Wright and Svetlana be disinterred, cremated and moved to Arizona to rest beside her. In a sign of the power Oglivanna held over the apprentices, even in death, without so much as a peep of protest they did exactly as she bid. Secretly, with the knowledge of only the Madison coroner who was legally required to agree to the cremation, the members of the Fellowship dug up Wright's body, had it cremated and carried the ashes to Taliesin West.

The outcries of shock and anger came quickly from Wright's family and friends – the children of Catherine and all of the original Taliesin apprentices were uniformly appalled – and from the State of Wisconsin, which threatened legal action against Arizona for an act one Wisconsin native described as equal to 'uprooting Jefferson from Monticello for reburial in Beverly Hills'. A Wisconsin state representative wrote, 'Much more than ashes have been taken from Wisconsin – the citizens of the state have lost one evidence of our history, spirit, and genius.' Most observers agree with Wright's son David, who felt that Oglivanna did it for purely selfish reasons, as 'she would be nobody without him'. There is also Oglivanna's jealousy of Mamah, arguably the great love of his life, lying next to him in the Unity Chapel graveyard for more than a quarter of a century. Yet his granddaughter Anne Baxter came closest to the deeper truth of the affair when she pointed out that Wright 'may be laughing for all we know, because his spirit is much bigger than his bones'.[35]

Epilogue:
Wright in the Rearview Mirror

In the late 1950s, shortly before Wright's death, Eero Saarinen responded to a question regarding Wright's importance to Modern architecture by saying, 'I think it may be that 50 years from now we will feel him stronger amongst us than right now. We are too close to him now . . . I think Wright's contribution has not yet been integrated into modern architecture.'[1] As Saarinen predicted 50 years ago, Wright's work is today being recognized as critical to the future of Modern architecture, in that it forms the heart of 'the other tradition of Modern architecture'[2] – those architects who define their discipline as centring on the conception and construction of an ethical and experiential framework for everyday life, grounded in its place, rather than its being determined by any extrinsic rationalization, universal formula or formal style. In this, Wright was the first architect to reverse the traditional American 'trade deficit' with Europe and the world with respect to architectural ideas of consequence.

Wright's architecture continues today to serve as a model for a humanist Modernism through its engagement of the tradition of practice and its integration of the poetic and the practical. In common with the great architects of the past, Wright believed that architectural form had moral meaning, that aesthetics and ethics were one and the same. Wright held that American democracy demanded integrity in the design and construction of architecture, as it required integrity in the individual citizen, and that internal values were invariably more important than external appearances. While this ideal of integrity has disappeared from the vast majority of buildings today, it remains embodied in the works of Wright and those architects who engage these same principles. Radical though it often may have appeared to his contemporaries, Wright argued that his architecture conserved and re-engaged the timeless disciplinary principles underlying the great buildings of the past, an inheritance giving insight into the fundamental nature of humankind.

It remains for us today to rediscover Wright's work and its countenance of principle, first perceived more than a century ago. Today, despite what appear to have been radical changes in design methods, building materials and functional programmes, every architect engages a discipline that has been fundamentally redefined by Wright: we are all affected by his work. For contemporary architects, Wright appears both behind us, as an *arriere-garde*, having reconnected the discipline of architecture to its ancient origins, and ahead of us, beyond any avant-garde, having anticipated somewhere in his enormous oeuvre every imaginable variation in the fundamental ordering principles of architecture.

Yet our universal insistence on only engaging architecture as a photograph in a book, or as an object to be viewed from the exterior, is in fact exactly the opposite of everything Wright believed about architecture. For Wright the inhabitation of a building, our experience of its interior spaces with all our senses, was the beginning of all architecture: it was only from this interior spatial experience that a building's external form was to be unfolded or projected. Wright's architecture itself was determined not by what it looked like on the outside, but by the use and comfort it provided its inhabitants in *the space within*. In order to truly understand Wright's architecture, it is never enough to read a book. One must inhabit his buildings and experience in the flesh these extraordinarily integrated and edifying places.

Wright believed that architecture should be the background or framework for daily life, and should never itself be the literal object of our attention – a remarkably modest definition from someone most often misrepresented as an arrogant maker of arbitrary forms. Yet Wright also believed that, in designing a building wherein human life *takes place*, architects accept the most significant ethical responsibilities and are obligated to attempt, to the best of their abilities, to improve the civilization, culture and place to which they belong. And Frank Lloyd Wright was an architect of astonishing ability, whose works and ideas continue to shape the world around us.

References

1 Unity and Nature's Geometry

1 Ada Louise Huxtable, *Frank Lloyd Wright* (New York, 2004), p. 1.
2 Brendan Gill, *Many Masks: A Life of Frank Lloyd Wright* (New York, 1987), p. 24.
3 Meryle Secrest, *Frank Lloyd Wright: A Biography* (New York, 1992), p. 29.
4 *Ibid.*, pp. 22–3.
5 Maginel Wright Barney, *The Valley of the God-Almighty Joneses* (New York, 1965). Book authored by Wright's sister.
6 Secrest, *Wright: A Biography*, p. 25.
7 *Ibid.*, p. 49.
8 Frank Lloyd Wright, *An Autobiography* (1932); ed. Bruce Brooks Pfeiffer, *Frank Lloyd Wright: Collected Writings, 1930–32* (New York, 1992), II, p. 109.
9 Huxtable, *Frank Lloyd Wright*, p. 6.
10 Wright, *An Autobiography* (1932); ed. Pfeiffer, II, p. 114.
11 Secrest, *Wright: A Biography*, p. 58; the quotation is from *As You Like It*, II.i.15–17.
12 Wright, *An Autobiography* (1932); ed. Pfeiffer, II, p. 113.
13 The Froebel quotations in this section are from Friedrich Froebel, *Selected Writings*, ed. I. M. Lilley (New York, 1898), pp. 160, 98.
14 Wright, *An Autobiography* (1932); ed. Pfeiffer, II, p. 111.
15 Norman Brosterman, *Inventing Kindergarten* (New York, 1997), pp. 104–31.
16 The Emerson quotations in this section are from Ralph Waldo Emerson, *Emerson's Essays* (New York, 1926), pp. 241, 105, 166, 60–61, 35, 41.
17 Frank Lloyd Wright, 'In the Cause of Architecture', *Architectural Review*, XXIII (1908), pp. 155–221; ed. Frederick Gutheim (New York, 1975), p. 123.
18 Charles Olson, *Call Me Ishmael* (San Francisco, 1947), pp. 11–12.

19 Henry David Thoreau, *Walden: or, Life in the Woods* (New York, 1985), p. 332.

20 David Michael Hertz, *Angels of Reality: Emersonian Unfoldings in Wright, Stevens and Ives* (Carbondale, IL, 1993), pp. 273, 286.

21 Wright, *An Autobiography* (1932); ed. Pfeiffer, II, pp. 142–3.

22 *Ibid.*, p. 145.

23 *Ibid.*, p. 146.

2 Chicago and the Tradition of Practice

1 Frank Lloyd Wright, *An Autobiography* (1932); ed. Bruce Brooks Pfeiffer, *Frank Lloyd Wright: Collected Writings, 1930–32* (New York, 1992), II, pp. 147–8.

2 David Van Zanten, *Sullivan's City* (New York, 2000), p. 23.

3 Wright, *An Autobiography* (1932); ed. Pfeiffer, II, p. 149.

4 Donald Miller, *City of the Century: The Epic of Chicago and the Making of America* (New York, 1996), pp. 335–8.

5 Wright, *An Autobiography* (1932); ed. Pfeiffer, II, pp. 165, 150.

6 Friedrich Froebel, *Selected Writings*, ed. I. M. Lilley (New York, 1898), p. 115.

7 Wright, *An Autobiography* (1932); ed. Pfeiffer, II, p. 152.

8 Joseph Connors, *The Robie House of Frank Lloyd Wright* (Chicago, 1984), p. 45.

9 Wright, *An Autobiography* (1932); ed. Pfeiffer, II, pp. 172, 152.

10 Louis Sullivan, *The Autobiography of an Idea* (New York, 1924, repr. 1956), p. 293.

11 Wright, *An Autobiography* (1932); ed. Pfeiffer, II, p.154.

12 Miller, *City of the Century*, p. 358.

13 *Ibid.*

14 Wright, *An Autobiography* (1932); ed. Pfeiffer, II, p. 165.

15 Sullivan, *Autobiography of an Idea*, pp. 206–10.

16 Miller, *City of the Century*, p. 303.

17 Anonymous reporter for the *Daily Inter-Ocean*, quoted in Van Zanten, *Sullivan's City*, p. 15.

18 All Greenough quotes are from Horatio Greenough, 'Form and Function', *A Memorial of Horatio Greenough*, ed. H. T. Tuckerman

(New York, 1853); repr. in Lewis Mumford, ed., *Roots of Contemporary American Architecture* (New York, 1972), pp. 39, 36, 38 and 37.

19 *Ibid.*, p. 33.

20 Louis Sullivan, 'Characteristics and Tendencies of American Architecture' (1885), reprinted in *Kindergarten Chats and Other Writings* (New York, 1979), pp. 177 and 182–3.

21 Wright, *An Autobiography* (1932); ed. Pfeiffer, II, p.172.

22 Kenneth Frampton, 'The Text-Tile Tectonic', in *On and By Frank Lloyd Wright: A Primer of Architectural Principles*, ed. Robert McCarter (New York, 2005), p. 172.

23 *Ibid.*, p. 176.

24 David Van Zanten, 'Kahn and Architectural Composition', unpublished paper read 24 January 2004, 'The Legacy of Louis I Kahn', Yale University.

25 Wright, *An Autobiography* (1932); ed. Pfeiffer, II, pp. 157–8.

26 Kevin Nute, *Frank Lloyd Wright and Japan* (New York, 1993), p. 22.

27 Wright, *An Autobiography* (1932); ed. Pfeiffer, II, pp. 174–5.

28 *Ibid.*, p. 132.

29 John Wellborn Root, *The Meanings of Architecture: Buildings and Writings by John Wellborn Root*, ed. Donald Hoffman (New York, 1967), p. 162.

30 Wright, *An Autobiography* (1932); ed. Pfeiffer, II, p. 190.

31 Patrick Pinnell, 'Academic Tradition and Individual Talent', in *On and By Frank Lloyd Wright*, ed. McCarter, p. 36.

3 White City and New World Monumentality

1 Frank Lloyd Wright, *An Autobiography* (1932), in *Frank Lloyd Wright: Collected Writings, 1930–32*, ed. Bruce Brooks Pfeiffer (New York, 1992), II, p. 185.

2 Leonard Eaton, *Two Chicago Architects and their Clients* (Cambridge, MA, 1969), pp. 25–63.

3 Donald Miller, *City of the Century: The Epic of Chicago and the Making of America* (New York, 1996), pp. 380–81.

4 *Ibid.*, p. 476.

5 *Ibid.*, pp. 381–4.

6 *Ibid.*, p. 488.

7 Quoted in Henry Steele Commager, *The American Mind* (New Haven,

CT, 1950), p. 396. Also cited in Alvin Rosenbaum, *Usonia: Frank Lloyd Wright's Design for America* (Washington, DC, 1993), pp. 34–5.

8 Erik Larson, *The Devil in the White City* (New York, 2003). Also a riveting account of Burnham's direction of the construction of the Exposition.

9 Kevin Nute, *Frank Lloyd Wright and Japan* (New York, 1993), p. 68.

10 *Ibid.*

11 Wright, *An Autobiography* (1932); ed. Pfeiffer, II, pp. 187–9.

12 Miller, *City of the Century*, p. 527.

13 John Lloyd Wright, *My Father Who is on Earth* (New York, 1946); repr. as *My Father, Frank Lloyd Wright* (New York, 1992), p. 30.

14 Miller, *City of the Century*, pp. 533–7.

15 H. Allen Brooks, *The Prairie School: Frank Lloyd Wright and his Midwest Contemporaries* (New York, 1976), p. 79.

16 Joseph Fenton, *Hybrid Buildings: Pamphlet Architecture No. 11* (New York, 1985) [catalogue of uniquely American type, with Chicago its birthplace].

17 Joseph Siry, *Unity Temple: Frank Lloyd Wright and Architecture for Liberal Religion* (Cambridge, MA, 1996), pp. 262–3.

18 Otto Antonia Graf, *Erraumen: Zum Werk von Frank Lloyd Wright*, III and IV (Vienna, 2002).

19 John Lloyd Wright, *My Father, Frank Lloyd Wright*, p. 22.

20 Patrick Meehan, ed., *Frank Lloyd Wright Remembered* (Washington, DC, 1991), p. 228.

21 Gwendolyn Wright, *Moralism and the Model Home: Domestic Architecture and Cultural Conflict in Chicago, 1873–1913* (Chicago, 1980).

22 Frank Lloyd Wright, 'The Architect and the Machine' (1894), 'Architect, Architecture, and the Client' (1896), in *Frank Lloyd Wright: Collected Writings, 1894–1930*, ed. Bruce Brooks Pfeiffer (New York, 1992), I, pp. 20–44.

23 *Ibid.*, p. 23.

24 Jack Quinan, *Frank Lloyd Wright's Martin House: Architecture as Portraiture* (New York, 2004).

25 Wright, *An Autobiography* (1932); ed. Pfeiffer, II, pp. 177–8.

26 John Lloyd Wright, *My Father, Frank Lloyd Wright*, pp. 31, 55–7.

4 Prairie House and the Progressive Movement

1 Patrick Pinnell, 'Academic Tradition and Individual Talent', in *On and By Frank Lloyd Wright: A Primer on Architectural Principles*, ed. Robert McCarter (London, 2005), pp. 49-54.

2 Colin Rowe, 'Chicago Frame', in *On and By Frank Lloyd Wright*, ed. McCarter, p. 89.

3 Frank Lloyd Wright, 'A Home in a Prairie Town' (1901), in *Frank Lloyd Wright: Collected Writings, 1894–1930*, ed. Bruce Brooks Pfeiffer (New York, 1992), I, pp. 73–5.

4 *Ibid.*, pp. 76–7.

5 Frank Lloyd Wright, 'Concerning Landscape Architecture' (1900), in *Wright: Collected Writings, 1894–1930*, ed. Pfeiffer, I , pp. 54–7.

6 David Van Zanten, *Sullivan's City* (New York, 2000), pp. 74–8.

7 John Lloyd Wright, *My Father Who is on Earth* (New York, 1946); repr. as *My Father, Frank Lloyd Wright* (New York, 1992), p. 27.

8 Frank Lloyd Wright, 'The Architect' (1900), in *Wright: Collected Writings, 1894–1930*, ed. Pfeiffer, I, pp. 49–50.

9 Frank Lloyd Wright, 'The Art and Craft of the Machine' (1901), in *Wright: Collected Writings, 1894–1930*, ed. Pfeiffer, II, pp. 58–69.

10 Leo Marx, *The Machine in the Garden: Technology and the Pastoral Ideal in America* (Oxford, 1964).

11 Joseph Connors, 'Wright and the Machine', *The Nature of Frank Lloyd Wright*, ed. C. Bolon, R. Nelson and L. Seidel (Chicago, 1998), p. 2.

12 All Hugo quotations are from Victor Hugo, *Notre Dame de Paris* (Paris, 1832; Eng. trans., New York, 1978), pp. 188–202.

13 Frank Lloyd Wright, 'The Art and Craft of the Machine' (1901); ed. Pfeiffer, II, p. 61.

14 Jane Addams, *Twenty Years at Hull House* (New York, 1910).

15 Robert Westbrook, *John Dewey and American Democracy* (Ithaca, NY, 1991), pp. 83, 382, 149, 402.

16 Thorstein Veblen, *The Theory of the Leisure Class* (New York, 1899).

17 Robert Ezra Park, *Human Communities* (Glencoe, IL, 1952), pp. 13, 5, 133, 59.

18 Wright, *An Autobiography* (1932), in *Frank Lloyd Wright: Collected Writings, 1894–1930*, ed. Bruce Brooks Pfeiffer (New York, 1992), II, p. 205.

19 Robin Evans, 'Figures, Doors and Passages', *Architectural Design* (April 1978), p. 278.

20 Jay Appleton, *The Experience of Landscape* (Chichester, 1975). Theory later applied to Wright's houses by Grant Hildebrandt, *The Wright Space* (Seattle, WA, 1991).

21 Leonard Eaton, *Two Chicago Architects and their Clients* (Cambridge, MA, 1969), pp. 128, 131.

22 Reyner Banham, *The Architecture of the Well-Tempered Environment* (London, 1969).

23 Wright, *An Autobiography* (1932); ed. Pfeiffer, II, pp. 199–200.

24 Wright, 'In the Cause of Architecture', *Architectural Review*, XXIII (1908), pp. 155–221; in *Wright: Collected Writings, 1894–1930*, ed. Pfeiffer, I, p. 86.

25 Richard Hofstadter, *The Age of Reform* (New York, 1955), p. 215.

26 Wright, 'Reply to Mr. Sturgis's Criticism' (1909), in Jack Quinan, *Frank Lloyd Wright's Larkin Building: Myth and Fact* (New York, 1987), p. 166.

27 Walt Whitman, 'Leaves of Grass' (1892), in *Walt Whitman: Poetry and Prose* (New York, 1982), p. 559.

28 Wright, *An Autobiography* (1932); ed. Pfeiffer, II, pp. 215–16.

29 Wright, 'The Architect' (1900), in *Wright: Collected Writings, 1894–1930*, ed. Pfeiffer, I, p. 51.

30 John Lloyd Wright, *My Father, Frank Lloyd Wright*, pp. 50–51.

31 As related by Wright's son, Llewelyn; Edgar Tafel, ed., *About Wright* (New York, 1993), p. 85.

32 Julia Meech, *Frank Lloyd Wright and the Art of Japan* (New York, 2001), pp. 40 and 58.

33 Wright, *An Autobiography* (1932); ed. Pfeiffer, II, pp. 219.

34 Grant Carpenter Manson, *Frank Lloyd Wright to 1910: The First Golden Age* (New York, 1958), p. 213.

5 Europe and the Shining Brow

1 The only comprehensive list of Wright's works, both projected and realized, assembled by Bruce Brooks Pfeiffer of the Frank Lloyd Wright Archives, is published in Robert McCarter, *Frank Lloyd Wright* (London, 1997), pp. 344–59.

2 Anthony Alofsin, *Frank Lloyd Wright: The Lost Years, 1910–22* (Chicago, 1993), p. 93.

3 *Ibid.*, p. 49.

4 Henry James, *Italian Hours* (1909), in *Henry James: Collected Travel Writings, The Continent* (New York, 1993), pp. 545, 409.

5 Andrew Saint, 'Wright and Great Britain', in *Frank Lloyd Wright: Europe and Beyond*, ed. Anthony Alofsin (Berkeley, CA, 1999), pp. 123–8.

6 Wright, 'The Japanese Print: An Interpretation' (1912), in *Frank Lloyd Wright: Collected Writings, 1894–1930*, ed. Bruce Brooks Pfeiffer (New York, 1992), I, p. 117.

7 Paul Kruty, *Frank Lloyd Wright and Midway Gardens* (Urbana, IL, 1998), p. 38.

8 Wright, *An Autobiography* (1932), in *Wright: Collected Writings, 1894–1930*, ed. Pfeiffer, II, pp. 230, 234, 237.

9 Wright, 'In the Cause of Architecture, Second Paper' (1914), in *Wright: Collected Writings, 1894–1930*, ed. Pfeiffer, I, pp. 137, 132.

10 Alofsin, *Wright: The Lost Years*, p. 225.

11 Edgar Tafel, ed., 'Robert Moses', *About Wright* (New York, 1993), p. 43.

12 Meryle Secrest, *Frank Lloyd Wright* (New York, 1992), p. 264.

13 Otto Antonia Graf, 'Enspacement: The Main Sequence from 4 to 6', *On and By Frank Lloyd Wright: A Primer of Architectural Principles*, ed. Robert McCarter (London, 2005), p. 145.

14 Gwendolyn Wright, 'Architectural Practice and Social Vision in Wright's Early Designs', *On and By Frank Lloyd Wright*, ed. McCarter, p. 102.

15 Wright, 'Chicago Culture' (1918), in *Wright: Collected Writings, 1894–1930*, ed. Pfeiffer, I, pp. 154–61.

6 Eastern Garden and Western Desert

1 Wright, *An Autobiography* (1932), in *Frank Lloyd Wright: Collected Writings, 1894–1930*, ed. Bruce Brooks Pfeiffer (New York, 1992), II, pp. 244–65.

2 John Lloyd Wright, *My Father Who is on Earth* (New York, 1946); repr. as *My Father, Frank Lloyd Wright* (New York, 1992), p. 96.

3 Wright, 'The New Imperial Hotel, Tokio' (1923), in *Wright: Collected Writings, 1894–1930*, ed. Pfeiffer, I, p. 177.

4 Wright, quoted in Norris Kelly Smith, *Frank Lloyd Wright: A Study in Architectural Content* (New York, 1966), p. 180.

5 Jun'ichiro Tanizaki, *In Praise of Shadows* (1933; Eng. trans., New Haven,

CT, 1977), pp. 38, 30.

6 Kathryn Smith, *Frank Lloyd Wright: Hollyhock House and Olive Hill* (New York, 1992), p. 17.

7 Wright, *An Autobiography* (1932), in *Wright: Collected Writings, 1894–1930*, ed. Pfeiffer, II, pp. 265. Brendan Gill, in a book filled with similar baseless accusations, has questioned the authenticity of this telegram from Okura, but the original copy at the F. L. Wright Archives confirms Wright's story; *Many Masks: A Life of Frank Lloyd Wright* (New York, 1987), p. 264.

8 Louis Sullivan, 'Concerning the Imperial Hotel' (1923), and 'Reflections on the Tokyo Disaster' (1924), in H. T. Wijdeveld, ed., *The Life Work of the American Artist Frank Lloyd* Wright (Santpoort, 1925); repr. as *The Work of Frank Lloyd Wright: The Wendingen Edition* (New York, 1965), II pp. 123, 131.

9 Wright, 'In the Cause of Architecture VIII: Sheet Metal and a Modern Instance' (1928), in *Wright: Collected Writings, 1894–1930*, ed. Pfeiffer, II, pp. 309.

10 Wright, 'The Pictures We Make' (1927), in *Wright: Collected Writings, 1894–1930*, ed. Pfeiffer, I, pp. 215, 218.

11 Lewis Mumford, 'The Social Background of Frank Lloyd Wright', in H. T. Wijdeveld, ed., *Work of Frank Lloyd Wright: Wendingen*, pp. 65–79.

12 Patrick Meehan, ed., 'Rev. Joseph A. Vaughan, SJ', *Frank Lloyd Wright Remembered* (Washington, DC, 1991), pp. 196–7.

13 Wright, 'Towards a New Architecture' (1928), in *Wright: Collected Writings, 1894–1930*, ed. Pfeiffer, I, pp. 317–18.

14 Wright, 'Fiske Kimball's New Book' (1928), *ibid.*, pp. 319–20.

15 Wright, 'Facts Regarding the Imperial Hotel' (1925), *ibid.*, p. 206.

16 Wright, 'Surface and Mass – Again!' (1929), *ibid.*, p. 326.

7 Fellowship and the Disappearing City

1 Joseph Connors, *The Robie House of Frank Lloyd Wright* (Chicago, 1984), p. 63.

2 John Dewey, 'From Absolutism to Experimentalism' (1930), *The Collected Works of John Dewey: The Later Works, 1925–1953*, ed. Jo Ann Boydston (Carbondale, IL, 1969–91), V, p. 160. Also quoted in Robert Westbrook,

John Dewey and American Democracy (Ithaca, NY, 1991), p. 462.

3 Wright, 'Poor Little American Architecture' (1930), in *Frank Lloyd Wright: Collected Writings, 1894–1930*, ed. Bruce Brooks Pfeiffer (New York, 1992), II, p. 17.

4 Woollcott, *The New Yorker* (19 July 1930); quoted in Meryle Secrest, *Frank Lloyd Wright* (New York, 1992), p. 374.

5 Wright, 'The Hillside Home School of the Applied Arts' (1931), in *Wright: Collected Writings, 1894–1930*, ed. Pfeiffer, III, p. 40.

6 Kenneth Frampton, 'Introduction', in *Wright: Collected Writings, 1894–1930*, ed. Pfeiffer, II, p. 7.

7 Wright, 'Modern Architecture: Being the Kahn Lectures' (1930), *ibid.*, pp. 20–79.

8 Wright, letter to E. Baldwin Smith, 8 February 1930, Frank Lloyd Wright Archives. Quoted in Kathryn Smith, 'The Show to End All Shows', *The Show to End All Shows*, ed. Peter Reed and William Kaizen (New York, 2004), p. 15.

9 Lewis Mumford, 'Two Chicago Fairs', *New Republic*, 65 (21 January 1931), p. 272. Quoted in Bruce Brooks Pfeiffer and Robert Wojtowicz, eds, *Frank Lloyd Wright and Lewis Mumford: Thirty Years of Correspondence* (New York, 2001), p. 15.

10 *Ibid.*, p. 123.

11 Wright, 'In the Cause of Architecture: A Confession' (1930), in *Wright: Collected Writings, 1894–1930*, ed. Pfeiffer, I, p. 347. 'Modern Architecture: Being the Kahn Lectures' (1930), *ibid.*, II, pp. 74–7.

12 Morton and Lucia White, *The Intellectual versus the City* (Oxford, 1962).

13 *Ibid.*, pp. 177–9.

14 Alvin Rosenbaum (*Usonia: Frank Lloyd Wright's Design for America* (Washington, DC, 1993), p. 108) believes Wright was given Wells's book in 1931 by the Willeys, his only house clients of this period.

15 Pfeiffer and Wojtowicz, eds, *Frank Lloyd Wright and Lewis Mumford*, pp. 117–18.

16 Rosenbaum, *Usonia*, pp. 100–101.

17 *Ibid.*, p. 106.

18 *Ibid.*, p. 105.

19 Wright, 'The Disappearing City' (1932), in *Wright: Collected Writings, 1894–1930*, ed. Pfeiffer, III, pp. 111–12.

20 *Ibid.*, p. 91.

21 Franklin Toker, *Fallingwater Rising* (New York, 2003), pp. 112–25.

22 Rosenbaum, *Usonia*, pp. 142–3.

23 Pfeiffer and Wojtowicz, eds, *Frank Lloyd Wright and Lewis Mumford*, pp. 164–6.

24 Wright, 'Architecture and Modern Life' (1937), in *Wright: Collected Writings, 1894–1930*, ed. Pfeiffer, III, p. 222.

25 Wright to Kaufmann, quoted by Bob Mosher and Donald Hoffmann, *Frank Lloyd Wright's Fallingwater* (New York, 1978), p. 17. Wright on Kaufmann in Wright, *The Future of Architecture* (New York, 1953), p. 16.

26 John Dewey, *Art as Experience* (New York, 1934), pp. 237, 212–13.

27 Interview with Og_livanna Wright, quoted in Jonathan Lipman, *Frank Lloyd Wright and the Johnson Wax Buildings* (New York, 1986), p. 15.

28 Wright, quoted *ibid.*, p. 93.

29 Meryle Secrest, *Frank Lloyd Wright: A Biography* (New York, 1992), p. 372.

30 Donald Johnson, *Frank Lloyd Wright versus America: The 1930s* (Cambridge, MA, 1990).

31 Secrest, *Frank Lloyd Wright*, p. 463.

32 Smith, in *The Show to End All Shows*, ed. pp. 29–30.

8 Natural House and the Fountainhead

1 Wright, 'The Natural House' (1954), in *Frank Lloyd Wright: Collected Writings, 1894–1930*, ed. Bruce Brooks Pfeiffer (New York, 1992), V, p. 102.

2 Wright, 'An Organic Architecture' (1939), in *Wright: Collected Writings, 1894–1930*, ed. Pfeiffer, III, pp. 317–18.

3 Patrick Meehan, ed., 'Samuel Freeman', 'Robert Berger' and 'John Howe', *Frank Lloyd Wright Remembered* (Washington, DC, 1991), pp. 63, 108, 133.

4 'Sarah Smith', 'Aaron G. Green', 'R. Buckminster Fuller', *ibid.*, pp. 95–6, 156, 41.

5 Edgar Tafel, ed., 'Carter H. Manny, Jr', *About Wright* (New York, 1993), p. 145.

6 Meehan, ed., 'John H. Howe', *Frank Lloyd Wright Remembered*, p. 129.

7 Tafel, ed., 'Marcus Weston', *About Wright*, p. 184.

8 'Yen Liang', *ibid.*, p. 130.

9 'Andrew Devane', 'William Wesley Peters', *ibid.*, pp. 120, 158.

10 Kathryn Smith, in Peter Reed and William Kaizen, ed., *The Show to End All Shows* (New York, 2004), p. 47.

11 Wright to Alan Reiach, Tafel's memory of Wright on the telephone, and Gropius; 'Alan Reiach', 'Walter Gropius', *ibid.*, pp. 173, 42–3, 45.

12 Wright, 'Of What Use is a Great Navy with No Place to Hide?' (1941), in *Wright: Collected Writings, 1894–1930*, ed. Pfeiffer, IV, p. 77.

13 Wright, 'Wake Up America!' (1940), *ibid.*, IV, p. 40.

14 Bruce Brooks Pfeiffer and Robert Wojtowicz, eds, *Frank Lloyd Wright and Lewis Mumford: Thirty Years of Correspondence* (New York, 2001), pp. 181–3.

15 Wright, 'Good Afternoon, Editor Evjue' (1941), 'Wake Up America!' (1940), 'An Open Letter to Patrick Stone' (1942), in *Wright: Collected Writings, 1894–1930*, ed. Pfeiffer, IV, pp. 79, 40, 105.

16 Tafel, ed., 'Henry Russell Hitchcock', *About Wright*, p. 224.

17 Wright, 'The New Frontier' (1940), in *Wright: Collected Writings, 1894–1930*, ed. Pfeiffer, IV, p. 64.

18 George Howe, 'Monuments, Memorials, and Modern Design', *Magazine of Art*, 37 (October 1944), pp. 202–7.

19 Alvar Aalto, letter to Aino Aalto, in Goran Schildt, *Alvar Aalto, The Mature Years* (New York, 1989), pp. 101–2.

20 Tafel, ed., 'William Wesley Peters', *About Wright*, pp. 163–4.

21 Meehan, ed., 'Walter Gropius', *Frank Lloyd Wright Remembered*, p. 46.

22 Robert Caro, *The Power Broker* (New York, 1975), p. 471.

23 Wright, 'To the Mole' (1944), in *Wright: Collected Writings, 1894–1930*, ed. Pfeiffer, IV, pp. 264–8.

24 Wright, 'Prejudice, Sir, is a Disease' (1947), *ibid.*, pp. 308–10.

25 Wright, 'AIA Acceptance Address' (1949), *ibid.*, pp. 325–30.

26 Meryle Secrest, *Frank Lloyd Wright: A Biography* (New York, 1992), p. 497.

9 Usonia Lost and Found

1 Wright, 'Whatever His Age . . . To the Young Man in Architecture' (1951), in *Frank Lloyd Wright: Collected Writings, 1894–1930*, ed. Bruce Brooks Pfeiffer (New York, 1992), V, p. 27. The philosopher referenced is Paul Ricoeur, 'Universal Civilization and National Cultures' (1961), *History and Truth* (Evanston, IL, 1965), pp. 271–86.

2 Wright, *A Testament* (1957), in *Wright: Collected Writings, 1894–1930*, ed.

Pfeiffer, v, p. 199.

3   Bruce Brooks Pfeiffer and Yukio Futagawa, eds, *Frank Lloyd Wright Monograph, 1942–1950* (Tokyo, 1988), p. 330.

4   Patrick Meehan, ed., 'Lewis Mumford', *Frank Lloyd Wright Remembered* (Washington, DC, 1991), p. 205.

5   Meryle Secrest, *Frank Lloyd Wright: A Biography* (New York, 1992), p. 539.

6   Wright, 'Force is Heresy' (1951), 'Wake Up Wisconsin' (1952), in *Wright: Collected Writings, 1894–1930*, ed. Pfeiffer, v, pp. 44, 51.

7   Wright, 'What American Government Should Do to Insure Lasting Peace in Korea' (1951), in *Wright: Collected Writings, 1894–1930*, ed. Pfeiffer, v, p. 42.

8   Bruce Brooks Pfeiffer and Robert Wojtowicz, eds, *Frank Lloyd Wright and Lewis Mumford: Thirty Years of Correspondence* (New York, 2001), pp. 216, 231, 233, 234.

9   Bruce Brooks Pfeiffer, introduction, 'Sixty Years of Living Architecture', in *Wright: Collected Writings, 1894–1930*, ed. Pfeiffer, v, p. 31.

10   Bruno Zevi, 'Wright and Italy: A Recollection', in *Frank Lloyd Wright: Europe and Beyond*, ed. Anthony Alofsin (Berkeley, CA, 1999), pp. 66–70.

11   *Ibid.*, pp. 72–3.

12   Pfeiffer, 'A Biographical Sketch,' in *Wright: Collected Writings, 1894–1930*, ed. Pfeiffer, v, p. 16.

13   Wright, 'Organic Architecture Looks at Modern Architecture' (1952), ibid., v, pp. 49–50.

14   Secrest, *Frank Lloyd Wright*, p. 551.

15   Edgar Tafel, ed., 'Frederick Gutheim', *About Wright* (New York, 1993), p. 220; Maginel Wright Barney, *The Valley of the God-Almighty Joneses* (New York, 1965), pp. 9–11.

16   Tafel, ed., 'Robert Moses', *About Wright*, pp. 41–4.

17   Lewis Mumford, 'The Sky Line: A Phoenix Too Infrequent', *The New Yorker* (I, 28 November 1953), p. 133, (II, 12 December 1953), pp. 125–7; reprinted in Lewis Mumford, *From the Ground Up* (New York, 1956), p. 75.

18   Pfeiffer and Wojtowicz, eds, *Frank Lloyd Wright and Lewis Mumford*, pp. 243, 248, 251.

19   Secrest, *Frank Lloyd Wright*, pp. 542–3.

20   Edgar Tafel, *Apprentice to Genius: Years with Frank Lloyd Wright* (New York, 1979), pp. 208–10.

21   Wright, 'The Solomon R. Guggenheim Museum' (1958), in *Wright:*

Collected Writings, 1894–1930, ed. Pfeiffer, v, pp. 245–8.

22 Herbert Muchamp, *Man about Town: Frank Lloyd Wright in New York City* (Cambridge, MA, 1983), p. 111.

23 Tafel, ed., 'Andy Rooney', *About Wright*, pp. 202–3.

24 Frank Lloyd Wright: The Mike Wallace Interviews', CBS/Archetype Associates, 1957, 1994.

25 Tafel, ed., 'Frederick Gutheim', *About Wright*, pp. 217–18.

26 John Dewey, *Art as Experience* (New York, 1934), p. 269.

27 Wright, 'Genius and the Mobocracy' (1949), in *Wright: Collected Writings, 1894–1930*, ed. Pfeiffer, IV, p. 382.

28 'Lewis Mumford,' excerpts from Mumford's autobiography, *Sketches from Life*, in Patrick Meehan, ed., *Frank Lloyd Wright Remembered* (Washington, DC, 1991), pp. 207–8.

29 Muchamp, *Man about Town*, pp. 184–5.

30 Kenneth Frampton, 'Introduction', in *Wright: Collected Writings, 1894–1930*, ed. Pfeiffer, IV, p. 9.

31 Wright, *The Natural House* (1954), in *Wright: Collected Writings, 1894–1930*, ed. Pfeiffer, IV, pp. 110–12.

32 Meehan, ed., 'Anne Baxter', *Frank Lloyd Wright Remembered*, pp. 241–2.

33 Secrest, *Frank Lloyd Wright*, p. 14.

34 Meehan, ed., 'Mies van der Rohe', *Frank Lloyd Wright Remembered*, p. 53.

35 All from Secrest, *Frank Lloyd Wright*: p. 17, Karl E. Meyer, *New York Times* (19 April 1985); p. 17, state representative in *Inland Architect*; p. 16, David Wright; p. 18, Anne Baxter.

Epilogue

1 Patrick Meehan, ed., 'Eero Saarinen' (1959), *Frank Lloyd Wright Remembered* (Washington, DC, 1991), p. 55.

2 Colin St John Wilson, *The Other Tradition of Modern Architecture* (London, 1995).

Bibliography

By Wright

An American Architecture (New York, 1955)

An Autobiography (New York, 1932, 1943, 1977)

Ausgefuhrte Bauten und Entwurfe von Frank Lloyd Wright (Berlin, 1910)

The Disappearing City (New York, 1932)

Drawings for a Living Architecture (New York, 1959)

Frank Lloyd Wright, Ausgefuhrte Bauten (Berlin, 1911)

Frank Lloyd Wright: Collected Writings, ed. Bruce Brooks Pfeiffer (New York):

    vol. I: *1894–1930* (1992)

    vol. II: *1930 –1932* (1992)

    vol. III: *1932–1939* (1993)

    vol. IV: *1939–1949* (1994)

    vol. V: *1949–1959* (1995)

Frank Lloyd Wright: On Architecture, ed. F. Gutheim (New York, 1941)

Frank Lloyd Wright: Writings and Buildings, ed. Edgar Kaufmann Jr and
    Ben Raeburn (New York, 1960)

The Future of Architecture (New York, 1953)

Genius and the Mobocracy (New York, 1949)

In the Cause of Architecture (essays, 1908–29), ed. F. Gutheim (New York, 1975)

The Japanese Print: An Interpretation (1912; repr. New York, 1967)

The Life-Work of Frank Lloyd Wright (Amsterdam, 1925)

The Living City (New York, 1958)

The Natural House (New York, 1954)

Sixty Years of Living Architecture (New York, 1953)

A Testament (New York, 1957)

When Democracy Builds (Chicago, 1945)

On Wright

Aguar, Charles E. and Berdeana, *Wrightscapes: Frank Lloyd Wright's Landscape Designs* (New York, 2002)

Alofsin, Anthony, ed., *Frank Lloyd Wright: An Index to the Taliesin Correspondence*, 5 vols (New York, 1998)

——, *Frank Lloyd Wright: Europe and Beyond* (Berkeley, CA, 1999)

——, *Frank Lloyd Wright: The Lost Years, 1910–22* (Chicago, 1993)

Bandes, Susan, ed., *Affordable Dreams: The Goetsch-Winkler House and Frank Lloyd Wright* (East Lansing, MI, 1991)

Birk, Melanie, ed., *Frank Lloyd Wright's Fifty Views of Japan* (San Francisco, 1996)

Blake, Peter, *Frank Lloyd Wright: Architecture and Space* (Harmondsworth, 1964)

Bolon, C., R. Nelson, and L. Seidel, (eds), *The Nature of Frank Lloyd Wright* (Chicago, 1988)

Brooks, Allen, ed., *Writings on Wright* (Cambridge, MA, 1981)

——, *The Prairie School: Frank Lloyd Wright and his Midwest Contemporaries* (New York, 1972)

Carter, Brian, *Johnson Wax Administration Building and Research Tower: Frank Lloyd Wright* (London, 1998)

Cleary, Richard, *Merchant Prince and Master Builder: Edgar J. Kaufmann and Frank Lloyd Wright* (Seattle, WA, 1999)

Connors, Joseph, *The Robie House of Frank Lloyd Wright* (Chicago, 1984)

De Long, David, *Auldbrass: Frank Lloyd Wright's Southern Plantation* (New York, 2003)

——, ed., *Frank Lloyd Wright: Designs for an American Landscape* (New York, 1996)

——, ed., *Frank Lloyd Wright and the Living City* (Milan, 1998)

Eaton, Leonard, *Two Chicago Architects and Their Clients* (Cambridge, MA, 1969)

Etlin, Richard, *Frank Lloyd Wright and Le Corbusier* (Manchester, 1994)

Futagawa, Yokio, and Bruce Brooks Pfeiffer, eds (Tokyo):

1 *Frank Lloyd Wright Monograph 1887–1901* (1986)

2 *Frank Lloyd Wright Monograph 1902–1906* (1987)

3 *Frank Lloyd Wright Monograph 1907–1913* (1987)

4 *Frank Lloyd Wright Monograph 1914–1923* (1985)

5 *Frank Lloyd Wright Monograph 1924–1936* (1985)

6 *Frank Lloyd Wright Monograph 1937–1941* (1986)

7 *Frank Lloyd Wright Monograph 1942–1950* (1988)

8 *Frank Lloyd Wright Monograph 1951–1959* (1988)

9 *Frank Lloyd Wright Preliminary Studies 1889–1916* (1985)

10 *Frank Lloyd Wright Preliminary Studies 1917–1932* (1986)

11 *Frank Lloyd Wright Preliminary Studies 1933–1959* (1987)

12 *Frank Lloyd Wright In His Renderings 1887–1959* (1984)

Futagawa, Yokio, ed., and Paul Rudolph, *Frank Lloyd Wright: Kaufmann House, 'Fallingwater'* (Tokyo, 1970)

——, ed., and Arata Isozaki, *Frank Lloyd Wright: Johnson and Son Administration Building and Research Tower* (Tokyo, 1970)

——, ed., and Bruce Brooks Pfeiffer, *Frank Lloyd Wright: Solomon Guggenheim Museum* (Tokyo, 1975)

——, ed., and Masami Tanigawa, *Frank Lloyd Wright: Taliesin East and Taliesin West* (Tokyo, 1975)

Gebhard, David and Scott Zimmerman, *Romanza: The California Architecture of Frank Lloyd Wright* (San Francisco, CA, 1988)

Graf, Otto Antonia, *Die Kunst des Quadrats: Zum Werk von Frank Lloyd Wright*, vols I and II (Vienna, 1983)

——, *Erraumen: Zum Werk von Frank Lloyd Wright*, vols III and IV (Vienna, 2002)

Gurda, John, *New World Odyssey, Annunciation Greek Orthodox Church and Frank Lloyd Wright* (Milwaukee, WI, 1986)

Hanks, David, *The Decorative Designs of Frank Lloyd Wright* (New York, 1979)

Hanna, Paul and Jean, *Frank Lloyd Wright's Hanna House* (Carbondale, IL, 1981)

Heinz, Thomas, *Dana House* (London, 1995)

——, *Frank Lloyd Wright* (New York, 1992)

Hertz, David Michael, *Angels of Reality: Emersonian Unfoldings in Wright, Stevens and Ives* (Carbondale, IL, 1993)

Hildebrandt, Grant, *The Wright Space: Pattern and Meaning in Frank Lloyd Wright's Houses* (Seattle, WA, 1991)

Hitchcock, Henry-Russell, *In the Nature of Materials: 1887–1941, The Buildings of Frank Lloyd Wright* (New York, 1941)

Hoffmann, Donald, *Frank Lloyd Wright: Architecture and Nature* (New York, 1986)

——, *Frank Lloyd Wright's Dana House* (New York, 1996)

——, *Frank Lloyd Wright's Fallingwater: The House and Its History* (New York, 1979, 1993)

——, *Frank Lloyd Wright's Hollyhock House* (New York: Dover, 1992)

——, *Frank Lloyd Wright's House on Kentuck Knob* (Pittsburgh, PA, 2000)

——, *Frank Lloyd Wright, Louis Sullivan and the Skyscraper* (New York, 1998)

——, *Frank Lloyd Wright's Robie House* (New York: Dover, 1984)

——, *Understanding Frank Lloyd Wright's Architecture* (New York, 1995)

Jacobs, Herbert and Katherine, *Building with Frank Lloyd Wright* (San Francisco, CA, 1978)

James, Cary, *The Imperial Hotel* (New York, 1993)

Johnson, Donald Leslie, *Frank Lloyd Wright versus America: The 1930s* (Cambridge, MA, 1990)

Kalec, David and Thomas Heinz, *Frank Lloyd Wright Home and Studio, Oak Park, Illinois* (Oak Park, IL, 1975)

Kaufmann Jr, Edgar, *Fallingwater: A Frank Lloyd Wright Country House* (New York, 1986)

——, *Nine Commentaries on Frank Lloyd Wright* (Cambridge, MA, 1989)

Kruty, Paul, *Frank Lloyd Wright and Midway Gardens* (Urbana, IL, 1998)

Levine, Neil, *The Architecture of Frank Lloyd Wright* (Princeton, NJ, 1996)

Lind, Karla, *Lost Wright* (New York, 1996)

Lipman, Jonathan, *Frank Lloyd Wright and the Johnson Wax Buildings* (New York, 1986)

Manson, Grant Carpenter, *Frank Lloyd Wright to 1910 : The First Golden Age* (New York, 1958)

McArthur, Shirley duFresne, *Frank Lloyd Wright: American System-Built Homes in Milwaukee* (Milwaukee, WI, 1983)

McCarter, Robert, *Fallingwater: Frank Lloyd Wright* (London, 1994)

——, *Frank Lloyd Wright* (London, 1997)

——, ed., *Frank Lloyd Wright: A Primer on Architectural Principles* (New York, 1991)

——, ed., *On and By Frank Lloyd Wright: A Primer of Architectural Principles* (London, 2005)

——, *Unity Temple: Frank Lloyd Wright* (London, 1997)

Meech, Julia, *Frank Lloyd Wright and the Art of Japan* (New York, 2001)

Meehan, Patrick, ed., *Frank Lloyd Wright Remembered* (Washington, DC, 1991)

——, ed., *Frank Lloyd Wright: A Research Guide to Archival Sources* (New York, 1983)

——, ed., *Truth Against the World: Frank Lloyd Wright Speaks for an Organic Architecture* (New York, 1987)

Menocal, Narcisco, ed., *Fallingwater and Pittsburgh*, Wright Studies, vol. 2 (Carbondale, IL, 2000)

——, ed., *Taliesin 1911–1914*, Wright Studies, vol. 1 (Carbondale, IL, 1992)

Muchamp, Herbert, *Man About Town: Frank Lloyd Wright in New York City* (Cambridge, MA, 1983)

Nute, Kevin, *Frank Lloyd Wright and Japan* (New York, 1993)

Patterson, Terry, *Frank Lloyd Wright and the Nature of Materials* (New York, 1994)

Pfeiffer, Bruce Brooks, and Robert Wojtowicz, *Frank Lloyd Wright + Lewis Mumford: Thirty Years of Correspondence* (New York, 2001)

Pfeiffer, Bruce Brooks, ed., *Frank Lloyd Wright: Drawings* (New York, 1990)

——, ed., *Frank Lloyd Wright: Letters to Apprentices* (New York, 1989)

——, ed., *Frank Lloyd Wright: Letters to Architects* (New York, 1989)

——, ed., *Frank Lloyd Wright: Letters to Clients* (New York, 1989)

——, *Frank Lloyd Wright: The Masterworks* (New York, 1993)

Quinan, Jack, *Frank Lloyd Wright's Larkin Building, Myth and Fact* (Cambridge, MA, 1987)

——, *Frank Lloyd Wright's Martin House: Architecture as Portraiture* (New York, 2004)

Reed, Peter and William Kaizen (eds), *The Show to End All Shows: Frank Lloyd Wright and the Museum of Modern Art, 1940* (New York, 2004)

Reisley, Roland, *Usonia, New York: Building a Community with Frank Lloyd Wright* (New York, 2001)

Riley, Terrance, ed., *Frank Lloyd Wright, Architect* (New York, 1994)

Rosenbaum, Alvin, *Usonia: Frank Lloyd Wright's Design for America* (Washington, DC, 1993)

Satler, Gail, *Frank Lloyd Wright's Living Space* (Dekalb, IL, 1999)

Scully, Vincent, *Frank Lloyd Wright* (New York, 1960)

Sergeant, John, *Frank Lloyd Wright's Usonian Houses* (New York, 1976)

Siry, Joseph, *Unity Temple: Frank Lloyd Wright and Architecture for Liberal Religion* (Cambridge, MA, 1996)

Sloan, Julie, *Light Screens: The Complete Leaded-Glass Windows of Frank Lloyd Wright* (New York, 2001)

Smith, Kathryn, *Frank Lloyd Wright: America's Master Architect* (New York, 1998)

——, *Frank Lloyd Wright: Hollyhock House and Olive Hill* (New York, 1992)
——, *Frank Lloyd Wright's Taliesin and Taliesin West* (New York, 1997)
Smith, Norris Kelly, *Frank Lloyd Wright, A Study in Architectural Content* (Englewood Cliffs, NJ, 1979)
Steele, James, *Barnsdall House: Frank Lloyd Wright* (London, 1992)
Storrer, William Allin, *The Architecture of Frank Lloyd Wright: A Complete Catalog* (Cambridge, MA, 1974)
——, *The Frank Lloyd Wright Companion* (Chicago, IL, 1993)
Sweeney, Robert, *Frank Lloyd Wright: An Annotated Bibliography* (Los Angeles, CA, 1978)
——, *Wright in Hollywood: Visions of a New Architecture* (Cambridge, MA, 1994)
Tafel, Edgar, ed., *About Wright* (New York, 1993)
——, *Apprentice to Genius: Years with Frank Lloyd Wright* (New York, 1979)
Toker, Franklin, *Fallingwater Rising: Frank Lloyd Wright, E.J. Kaufmann, and America's Most Extraordinary House* (New York, 2003)
Zevi, Bruno, *Frank Lloyd Wright* (Bologna, 1979)

Biographies

Barney, Maginel Wright, *The Valley of the God-Almighty Joneses* (New York, 1965)
Gill, Brendan, *Many Masks: A Life of Frank Lloyd Wright* (New York, 1987)
Hoppen, Donald, *The Seven Ages of Frank Lloyd Wright* (New York, 1998)
Huxtable, Ada Louise, *Frank Lloyd Wright* (New York, 2004)
Jacobs, Herbert, *Frank Lloyd Wright: America's Greatest Architect* (New York, 1965)
Secrest, Meryle, *Frank Lloyd Wright* (New York, 1992)
Twombley, Robert, *Frank Lloyd Wright: An Interpretive Biography* (New York, 1973)
Wright, John Lloyd, *My Father Who Is On Earth* (New York, 1946)

Acknowledgements

The writing of a biography involves not only research, but selection, for one can never tell the whole story. This is the story of Wright's life as an architect, told by an architect, focusing on Wright's practice of a discipline that is inherently and inextricably bound up in the social, economic, material, environmental, political, philosophical and cultural circumstances of its time and place. For Wright, the tradition of practice involved not a distancing from the commonplace, but rather an ethical engagement of the everyday, a five-fingered grasp of reality that assured that his works were fully integrated into the life-world. While this selective story of Wright's life is entirely my responsibility, I would like to acknowledge several important influences on my 'other' life as a writer. Vivian Constantinopoulos, who encouraged me to enter what was for me the new territory of biography. Kenneth Frampton, whose insistence that Wright's work continues to be of critical importance to the future of architecture has deeply affected my generation of architects. Joseph Connors, who never allowed me to forget that architecture comes from both creative thought and its social, political, cultural and physical circumstance. Finally, this book is dedicated to Bruce Brooks Pfeiffer, whose life-work has assured that the records of Wright's process and practice will be available for all those who follow in Wright's wake.

Photographic Acknowledgements

The author and publishers wish to express their thanks to the below sources of illustrative material and/or permission to reproduce it:

Photos courtesy of the author: pp. 78 (top), 85, 129, 134, 135, 140, 145, 153 (top); photo Chicago Historical Society: p. 149; photos in the collection of the Frank Lloyd Wright Preservation Trust, Oak Park, Illinois: pp. 11 (H&S H203), 86 (H&S H132); photos courtesy The Frank Lloyd Wright Archives, Taliesin West, Scottsdale, Arizona: pp. 29, 40, 66, 91, 94, 105, 111, 112, 116, 117, 128, 132, 152, 189; photo courtesy of the Avery Architectural and Fine Arts Library, Columbia University, New York: p. 153 (foot); photo courtesy of S. C. Johnson & Son, Inc.: p. 138; photo Library of Congress, Washington, DC (Prints and Photographs Division, LC-USZ62-36384): p. 6; photo Ragghianti Archives, Archivio "Sele Arte", Florence: p. 178; photo Wisconsin State Historical Society: p. 199; plan and photos from Frank Lloyd Wright, *Frank Lloyd Wright: Ausgefuhrte Bauten* (Berlin, 1911): pp. 56, 69, 77, 78 (foot), 81, 83.